M. Fatih Elaziz

Student and Teacher Attitudes to Interactive Whiteboards in EFL Class

M. Fatih Elaziz

Student and Teacher Attitudes to Interactive Whiteboards in EFL Class

A survey and observation investigating the use and the attitudes of students and teachers in language classes

LAP LAMBERT Academic Publishing

Impressum/Imprint (nur für Deutschland/only for Germany)
Bibliografische Information der Deutschen Nationalbibliothek: Die Deutsche
Nationalbibliothek verzeichnet diese Publikation in der Deutschen Nationalbibliografie;
detaillierte bibliografische Daten sind im Internet über http://dnb.d-nb.de abrufbar.
Alle in diesem Buch genannten Marken und Produktnamen unterliegen warenzeichen-,
marken- oder patentrechtlichem Schutz bzw. sind Warenzeichen oder eingetragene
Warenzeichen der jeweiligen Inhaber. Die Wiedergabe von Marken, Produktnamen,
Gebrauchsnamen, Handelsnamen, Warenbezeichnungen u.s.w. in diesem Werk berechtigt
auch ohne besondere Kennzeichnung nicht zu der Annahme, dass solche Namen im Sinne
der Warenzeichen- und Markenschutzgesetzgebung als frei zu betrachten wären und
daher von jedermann benutzt werden dürften.

Coverbild: www.ingimage.com

Verlag: LAP LAMBERT Academic Publishing GmbH & Co. KG
Heinrich-Böcking-Str. 6-8, 66121 Saarbrücken, Deutschland
Telefon +49 681 3720-310, Telefax +49 681 3720-3109
Email: info@lap-publishing.com

Approved by: Ankara, Bilkent University, Diss., 2008

Herstellung in Deutschland (siehe letzte Seite)
ISBN: 978-3-659-12476-1

Imprint (only for USA, GB)
Bibliographic information published by the Deutsche Nationalbibliothek: The Deutsche
Nationalbibliothek lists this publication in the Deutsche Nationalbibliografie; detailed
bibliographic data are available in the Internet at http://dnb.d-nb.de.
Any brand names and product names mentioned in this book are subject to trademark,
brand or patent protection and are trademarks or registered trademarks of their respective
holders. The use of brand names, product names, common names, trade names, product
descriptions etc. even without a particular marking in this works is in no way to be
construed to mean that such names may be regarded as unrestricted in respect of
trademark and brand protection legislation and could thus be used by anyone.

Cover image: www.ingimage.com

Publisher: LAP LAMBERT Academic Publishing GmbH & Co. KG
Heinrich-Böcking-Str. 6-8, 66121 Saarbrücken, Germany
Phone +49 681 3720-310, Fax +49 681 3720-3109
Email: info@lap-publishing.com

Printed in the U.S.A.
Printed in the U.K. by (see last page)
ISBN: 978-3-659-12476-1

ATTITUDES OF STUDENTS AND TEACHERS TOWARDS THE USE OF INTERACTIVE
WHITEBOARDS IN EFL CLASSROOMS

The Graduate School of Education of
Bilkent University

by

M. FATİH ELAZİZ

In Partial Fulfilment of the Requirements for the Degree of
MASTER OF ARTS

in

THE DEPARTMENT OF
TEACHING ENGLISH AS A FOREIGN LANGUAGE
BILKENT UNIVERSITY
ANKARA

September 2008

ABSTRACT

ATTITUDES OF STUDENTS AND TEACHERS TOWARDS THE USE OF INTERACTIVE
WHITEBOARDS IN EFL CLASSROOMS

M. Fatih Elaziz

M. A., Department of Teaching English as a Foreign Language

Supervisor: Asst. Prof. Dr. Julie Mathews Aydınlı

July 2008

This study explored the attitudes of students, teachers, and administrators towards the use of interactive whiteboards (IWBs) in language teaching and learning contexts, and also sought insights into students' and teachers' actual use of IWBs in English as a foreign language classes. The study also investigated possible factors affecting teachers' and students' positive and negative attitudes towards IWB technology.

Data were collected through questionnaires distributed to 458 students and 82 teachers in different institutions across Turkey, ranging from primary schools to universities. Three administrators were interviewed in order to explore their opinions towards IWB use in language instruction, and three classrooms were observed. Questionnaire results revealed that both students and teachers have positive attitudes towards the use of IWBs in language instruction and are aware of the potential of this technology. Responses given in interviews indicated that all administrators are supportive of IWB technology in English classes, and observations revealed that IWBs are used with their basic functions in English classes. The statistical analysis revealed that the more teachers use IWBs, the more they like this technology. It was also found that as the number of hours of IWB exposure increases, students' awareness of the distinctiveness of IWB technology rises.

Key words: Interactive whiteboard (IWB), attitude.

ACKNOWLEDGEMENTS

I would like to express my gratitude to my thesis advisor, Asst. Prof. Dr. Julie Mathews Aydınlı, for her invaluable guidance, encouragement, and support throughout my study and the program. Her assistance and contributions helped me to deal with the painstaking thesis writing process and get a better job in my study. Being one of her advisees and students is a real privilege for me.

I am also indebted to Asst. Prof. Dr. JoDee Walters for her contributions and guidance for my thesis. I owe much to her for her valuable support, encouragement, kindness, and suggestions not only for my thesis, but also the courses I took throughout the year.

I owe special thanks to Prof. Dr. Alinur Büyükaksoy, the Rector of Gebze Institute of Technology and Asst. Prof. Dr. Engin Başaran, for their encouragement regarding academic studies and giving me permission to attend this program. I also thank to Asst. Prof. Dr. Hüseyin Altay for his help with statistics and support.

I would like to thank my friends Ramazan Alparslan Gökçen and Adem Al for their contributions and encouragement sharing their knowledge and experience with me.

I owe special thanks to my dearest sister, Aliye Elaziz, for motivating me all the time and tolerating me throughout the year. I am also grateful to my mother, my father, my brother, and my elder sister. Without their love, affection, and encouragement, I would not be able to succeed in life.

TABLE OF CONTENTS

6

LIST OF TABLES

Table

CHAPTER I: INTRODUCTION

Introduction

With the introduction of computer facilities into the education system, traditional teaching techniques are increasingly being enhanced or even replaced by techniques relying more on technology. Once concentrated in math and science classes, technology has also begun providing benefits to language teaching and learning. One recent popular computer based technology that has emerged is interactive whiteboards (IWBs). IWBs were initially developed for presentations in office settings, but over the last decade, starting from higher education, educational institutions have begun using them. According to some studies and reports based primarily on research in science, math or other content-based classrooms, the use of IWBs makes the learning and teaching atmosphere more enjoyable, creative, and interesting. There are also numerous claims about the benefits and positive impact of IWBs on learning, but these remain largely anecdotal.

With the incorporation of IWBs in teaching and learning settings, important changes have been observed in education, such as engaging more students in the lesson, using multimedia sources flexibly, and motivating learners easily. IWBs could be useful supplementary tools for education, providing the opportunity to bring in different kinds of multimedia resources, to access Internet sources with ease, and to increase student interest; however, maximum benefit from this technology, especially in language teaching and learning settings, requires further background knowledge and research. Although there are many descriptive reviews and reports about the use of IWBs, it is beneficial for teachers and students to be familiar with the actual potential of this technology through empirical studies, including gathering the opinions of students and teachers, exploring its actual use in the classroom, and providing pedagogical advice for effective use of this technology.

Background of the Study

In recent years, computers and computer-related technologies, such as IWBs, have increasingly begun to be used in language teaching and learning settings. Technologically developed countries such as the UK, the USA, and Australia have invested a great deal of money in such technological equipment. With respect to IWBs in particular, a national survey in England in 2005 found that nearly half (49%) of primary school teachers had used IWBs, and in secondary schools, 77% of math teachers, 67% of science teachers and 49% of English teachers said they had used IWBs (BECTA, 2005). In financial terms, this has meant that in a recent five year period £50 million was spent on IWBs (DfES, 2004b). There is increasing interest in the potential of this technology worldwide (Bell, 2002; Hodge & Anderson, 2007; Kent, 2004), including in countries

9

like Turkey, where, though this technology is quite new, it is attracting educators' attention day by day.

Interactive whiteboards have been argued to provide certain benefits for students. Firstly, using IWBs has been claimed to increase student motivation and enjoyment (BECTA, 2003a). Secondly, they have been shown to enable greater opportunities for participation and collaboration, thus developing students' personal and social skills (Levy, 2002). Thirdly, they may eliminate the need for students to take notes, through the capacity to save and print what appears on the board (BECTA, 2003b). Another benefit is arguably that, with the help of an IWB, teachers can make clearer and more dynamic presentations and in turn the students can manage to deal with more complex concepts (Smith, 2001). It has also been argued that IWBs allow teachers to accommodate different learning styles and to choose materials according to the particular needs of students (Bell, 2002). Moreover, IWBs seem to enable students to be more creative and self-confident in presentations to their classmates (Levy, 2002). Finally, Bell suggests using IWBs for a variety of reasons. Since IWBs are colorful tools, they attract the attention of students and they may be useful not only for visual intelligent students, but also for kinesthetic learners because they allow touching and marking on the board.

IWBs may provide benefits for teachers as well. First of all, IWBs have been shown to provide teachers with a way to integrate Information and Communication Technology (ICT) into their lessons while teaching from the front of the class (Smith, 2001). Secondly, they may allow for spontaneity and flexibility, and for teachers to benefit from a wide range of web-based resources (Kennewell, 2001). Thirdly, they permit teachers to save and print the notes they or their students write on the board (Walker, 2002). Furthermore, IWBs allow teachers to share materials with their colleagues via intranet at schools and use them again later, which saves time in preparing materials (Glover & Miller, 2001). Finally, interactive whiteboards have been argued to serve as encouraging devices for teachers to change their pedagogical approaches and use more ICT, which in turn can facilitate professional development (Smith, 1999).

Even though there are many reports claiming to show the advantages of IWBs, there are also a few studies pointing out the drawbacks of this technology. In a study conducted by Gray, Hagger-Vaughan, Pilkington and Tomkins (2005), researchers found that some teachers complained that IWB-based lesson preparation and planning is time-consuming. Other teachers stated that too much Powerpoint use could lead to a "show and tell" style of teaching that may result in changing the role of the teacher into one of just a presenter of the topic in the classroom. In this case, the teacher may be seen as more passive and as less involved in the teaching process. Smith, Higgins, Wall and Miller (2005) revealed that in order to use IWBs to their full potential and avoid such problems,

10

there is a tremendous need for training and technical support for teachers. Teachers should be confident in using this technology, which can only be achieved by special training. Without training, the claimed benefits may not be experienced by the learners and teachers. Glover and Miller (2001) conducted another study that supports this idea, emphasizing many teachers' lack of overall ICT competence. Yet another problem that may arise with the introduction of IWB technology is a financial one. Schools have to spend a considerable amount of money in order to equip classrooms with this technology. Yet, if there are only one or two classrooms equipped with IWBs, students and teachers may suffer from inadequate access to IWB technology (Smith, 1999).

With all these claimed benefits and possible disadvantages of IWBs, what do those who use them think about them? To explore the attitudes of students and teachers towards the use of IWBs, a few studies in different content classes have been conducted, such as Glover and Miller (2001), Lee and Boyle (2004), Hall and Higgins (2005), and Kennewell and Morgan (2003). Aside from generally reporting positive attitudes on the parts of students and teachers alike towards IWBs, these attitude studies have provided important information to help educators form informed and scientifically supported opinions about this new technology - a crucial first step with any new innovation in educational settings.

Statement of the Problem

Since the late 1990s there has been an increasing use of technology in educational settings worldwide. Computer facilities such as wireless net, interactive whiteboards, and multimedia devices have started to enhance teaching and learning processes. Interactive whiteboards (IWBs) are a relatively recent technology, so there is not a great deal of scholarly literature relating to attitudes towards their use. The articles in the educational press and newspapers offer only anecdotal evidence and advice and the existing small-scale studies do not provide a full picture - particularly with respect to IWB use in the area of language instruction.

Various studies have investigated the attitudes of students and teachers towards CALL (Arkın, 2003; Bebell, O'Conner, O'Dwyer, & Russell, 2003; Lin, 2001; Passey & Rogers, 2004; Pekel, 1997; Tuzcuoğlu, 2000) and several studies have looked at the student and teachers attitudes towards the use of interactive whiteboards in particular (Glover & Miller, 2001; Gray et al., 2005; Hall & Higgins, 2005; Kennewell & Morgan, 2003; Lee & Boyle, 2004; Levy, 2002; Moss, Jewitt, Levaãiç, Armstrong, Cardini, Castle, 2007; Schmid, 2006; Wall, Higgins, Smith, 2005). Of the latter studies only two looked specifically at IWB use in language learning contexts (Gray et al., 2005; Schmid, 2006), and of these, both were small-scale qualitative studies looking at specific groups of ESL learners and teachers. The literature lacks therefore large-scale studies surveying

11

specifically language teachers', learners', and administrators' views about the use of IWBs in EFL contexts and exploring the possible factors affecting these stakeholders' positive or negative attitudes towards IWB technology.

In Turkey, IWB technology is fairly new and there are not many institutions that use it currently for language teaching purposes. Since research studies may be helpful to educators deciding whether or not to invest in this new technology, this study will be a starting point to show the overall picture of IWB use in Turkey, student and teacher openness to their use, and their overall potential for language instruction. This study will include all of the stakeholders in language instruction settings by exploring teachers', students', and administrators' attitudes both qualitatively and quantitatively, so that educators may decide whether they should incorporate this technology into their teaching process or not.

Research Questions

1) What are the attitudes of Turkish EFL teachers towards interactive whiteboards?

2) What are the attitudes of Turkish EFL students towards interactive whiteboards?

3) What are the attitudes of administrators in Turkish educational contexts towards interactive whiteboards?

4) How are IWBs used in EFL classrooms in Turkey?

5) What factors may influence Turkish students' and teachers' attitudes towards the use of IWBs in EFL classrooms?

Significance of the Study

IWB technology is becoming more and more widespread day by day since it appears to offer teachers and students opportunities to facilitate teaching and learning. Although there are many claimed benefits of IWB technology, it is the teachers who will have to exploit the features of IWBs and integrate them with their current teaching methodologies, and students who will be expected to be ready for such changes. Effective integration can be achieved once it is understood how much training is needed, how open teachers and students are to the idea of IWB use, and how much support can be expected from administrators. Since the literature lacks broad empirical studies investigating students' and teachers' attitudes towards IWB technology in language instruction, this study might provide more empirical results, including both qualitative and quantitative data, showing how language teachers and EFL students perceive IWB technology, and ultimately may help both teachers and students maximise the benefits of IWB technology.

This is the first study that will investigate the attitudes of students, teachers, and administrators towards the use of IWBs in language instruction settings in Turkey. Before deciding

12

on whether to invest in any new technology, educators need to understand how much this technology may contribute to their particular teaching and learning process, and need to be aware of opinions of the people who are using this technology currently. This study will enable Turkish educational institutions in the language teaching field to make informed decisions about whether to invest in this technology, and to better understand what they need to do if they decide to make this commitment.

Conclusion

This chapter gave a brief summary of the literature about IWBs in education. As is clear from the literature, more studies are needed to examine the attitudes of students, teachers, and administrators in language teaching and learning settings. Additionally, the actual use of IWBs in current institutions where IWBs are used in English classes and the factors affecting the attitudes of students and teachers also require further investigation. The next chapter provides a more in-depth review of the literature on computer-assisted language learning, the use of interactive whiteboards, the benefits and drawbacks of IWBs, and research on the attitudes of students and teachers towards IWBs. The third chapter presents information about the current study's participants and setting, instruments, and procedures followed to collect and analyze the data. The fourth chapter is comprised of the procedures for data analysis and the results of the survey study. The last chapter presents a discussion of the findings, pedagogical implications, limitations, and suggestions for further research.

CHAPTER II: LITERATURE REVIEW

Introduction

Over the past several decades, technology has become a fixture in many homes around the world, and it has influenced all facets of our lives, including education. The rapidly increasing use of computer technology and CALL has been argued to make language teaching and learning more enjoyable, effective, and versatile. Word processors, using websites, email, chat, online tutoring, blogs, podcasts, concordancers, and interactive whiteboards are some of the CALL applications that are commonly employed by teachers and students. Since the late 1990s, interactive whiteboards (IWBs) have started to be installed in classrooms, especially in the UK, the USA, and Australia. Today, technologically developing countries are also becoming more interested in IWB technology and are trying to install this technology in as many schools as possible. Recent research reports and findings reveal a mixed picture about the potential of IWBs. On the one hand, there are reports and newspaper articles that identify how IWBs are beneficial, effective, motivating, and facilitating (e.g. Bell, 2002; Harris, 2005; Smith, 2001; Walker, 2002). On the other hand, others suggest that the mere introduction of such technologies is insufficient to enhance learning to a large extent and that IWBs' impact should be investigated more with empirical studies (Gray et al., 2005; Smith et al., 2005).

This chapter will first give a general background of CALL, followed by the advantages, and then disadvantages of CALL in terms of both students and teachers. Next, the definition, benefits and drawbacks of interactive whiteboards will be explained according to the previous studies and reports. Finally, attitudes and perceptions of students and teachers towards the use of IWB technology will be presented.

Technology in the Classroom

The Emergence of CALL

The history of the first computers used in language teaching and learning settings dates back to the 1950s and the 1960s (Beatty, 2003). The computers in that era were very large and expensive, and primarily used for research in laboratories. As we know, before the invention of CD-ROMs, DVDs and microcomputers, audio cassettes and video tapes were the primary forms of "technology" used for language teaching and learning purposes. With these later inventions, more information was able to be technologically stored and carried to different places (Beatty, 2003). Additionally, educational computing spread through government-funded projects such as PLATO (Programmed Logic for Automatic Teaching Operations) in the 1960s. PLATO was designed to provide interactive, self-paced instruction for large numbers of students and integrated text and

14

graphics, and was thus a kind of restricted e-mail system (Alessi & Trollip, 1991; Levy, 1997). Computers became widely available to language teachers in the early 1980s due to a drop in prices that accompanied the invention of microcomputers (Chapelle, 2001; Levy, 1997). These microcomputers allowed interaction through text, graphics, voice, and pointing along with the ease of using audio and visual devices (Alessi & Trollip, 1991). Early CALL programs were based on texts and enabled learners to carry out simple tasks such as gap filling, matching sentence halves, and answering multiple-choice questions (Dudeney & Hockly, 2007). Highly-motivated language teachers started to write their own CALL programs using BASIC (Beginner's All-purpose Symbolic Instruction Code), which played an important role in improving CALL materials (Levy, 1997).

In the early 1980s, there was considerable effort placed upon the pedagogical impact of computers in education by some academicians and educators. In 1983, the annual Teachers of English to Speakers of Other Languages (TESOL) conference included papers arguing on methodological issues in CALL and a suggestion was made by the academicians to establish a professional organization (CALICO) (Chapelle, 2001). People working on CALL wanted to be more organized among themselves and tried to attract educators' attention to CALL and its uses in language instruction. By the late 1980s, CALL had developed through a number of ambitious projects such as the investigation of field-independent learners' performance with CALL and their attitudes towards CALL (Ahmad, Corbett, Rogers & Sussez, 1985; Chapelle, 2001). Multimedia also attracted educators' attention after the late 1980s because of the notion that it helps to stimulate the senses, and increase involvement, attention, and concentration (Chapelle, 2001)

By the middle of the 1990s, a major breakthrough occurred with the evolution of the World Wide Web (www), which allowed students and teachers to reach a wide variety of Internet resources including audio, visual, and textual materials (Boswood, 1997; Levy, 1997). With the spread of Information and Communications Technology (ICT) to larger groups of people, CALL moved beyond the use of computer programs to integrate with the Internet and web-based tools (Dudeney & Hockly, 2007). After the development of Internet facilities and the rapid growth of computer sales for personal and professional purposes, teachers and students started to benefit from the facilities of the Internet and other information technologies, both in classrooms and in their homes. Although the use of ICT by language teachers is still not very widespread in many countries, there is a growing interest in computer technology among language teachers. As the Internet provides authentic tasks and materials, ready-made ELT materials, the opportunity to participate in distance-learning contexts, and new ways of practicing language skills (Pennington, 1996; Smith, 1997; Warschauer, 2000), it is inevitable that teachers will become accustomed to using computers in and outside the classrooms.

15

Use of CALL in Language Teaching

In recent decades, student-centered methodologies have gained importance and teachers have started to change their traditional ways of teaching. Since students have increasingly become the center of education, they have begun to be held more responsible for their own learning, which has resulted in a greater emphasis on autonomous learners (Kenning & Kenning, 1983). With the use of CALL, real language use in a meaningful and authentic context is possible, integrating various skills, such as listening, speaking, writing, and reading (Lee, 2000; Warschauer & Healey, 1998). Today, use of multimedia-based materials and the Internet provide a great deal of informational, authentic, and communicative sources and activities for every student (Lee, 2000). Therefore, both students and teachers should have an idea about the benefits of CALL and be selective in choosing and using appropriate CALL programs and materials for language teaching and learning. This section will first focus on the advantages of CALL from the perspective of students and then from the perspective of teachers.

Advantages of CALL for Students

CALL offers a number of advantages for students such as independent practice, interactivity, private learning (Kenning & Kenning, 1983), independent pacing, immediate feedback, and the opportunity to edit work (Ahmad et al., 1985). All these features may influence learners to be more motivated, self-confident, and independent in the learning process (Schoepp & Eroğul, 2001). Once students are trained how to benefit from computer-based materials and the Internet in particular, they can reach authentic materials easily and develop their language skills with a variety of resources according to their own pace of learning.

According to Kenning and Kenning (1983), computers offer privacy to learners, allowing them to work on their own computers and preventing other students from seeing their work and thereby preventing them from any feelings of humiliation. In this case, the affective filters of the learners, such as anxiety, fear, and nervousness, are lowered. Computers also enable individual work, which provides learners an opportunity to decide the pace of learning and the study period by themselves. For instance, if someone is a slow learner, he/she may focus on all the exercises or drills on a subject, find related materials from the Internet, and work with them according to his/her choice. By contrast, in an actual classroom setting, teachers would not likely have an opportunity to review the entire subject to accommodate slow learners because of time and syllabus constraints. Kenning and Kenning (1983) also differentiate between other technological devices, such as tape-recorders, videos, projectors, and computers, according to the type of the interaction required or enabled. Computers can interact with learners in different ways such as correcting a mistake, checking pronunciation by recording the voice, and indicating the wrong answer with sound, whereas a tape can only provide the recorded material without interaction with the learner.

Costanzo (1989) and Ahmad et al. (1985) point out that the computer's infinite patience is another great advantage for students. Learners can spend hours practicing linguistic forms, writing tests, and composing new documents on the computer since the computer does not have the same time constraints that a teacher faces. Computers also have another advantage related to the way the questions are asked. The learners may not ask questions in the classroom just because of their shyness, but they can ask a lot of questions to other people on the computer or to the software by using the keyboard (Ahmad et al., 1985; Lee, 2000).

Recently, more and more CALL software programs are appearing on the market. One of the most important advantages of these programs is to be able to give feedback to the learners immediately and correctly (Jung & Kim, 2004). Getting correct and immediate feedback is essential for learners because they want to measure their progress and obtain answers in a short time. Unlike with teachers, computers can give learners the opportunity to receive feedback very soon, so the learners do not depend on teachers (Robinson, 1991).

In writing classes, computers can also be very useful. By using a word processing program such as Microsoft Word, learners can create their own compositions, store them on a portable flash disk so that they can read and edit their work at home, see their spelling mistakes, and insert images and graphics into their written texts to make them more visually interesting (Dudeney & Hockly, 2007). It is also possible for learners to write and send their drafts to their teachers via the internet and teachers may give feedback by using TrackChanges through which the learners see some suggestions for correction and improvement for the next draft (Dudeney & Hockly, 2007).

Turning to the Internet in particular, we see that it has been argued to enrich our language learning settings (Vilmi, 1999). It can provide a huge amount of resources not only for learners but also for teachers. Since it is the world's largest library and an unlimited virtual realm, learners can use it for searching for specific information, testing their language skills, chatting with native speakers, listening to online radio and other programs, getting online tutoring, downloading materials and so on (BECTA, 2004; Shin & Son, 2007). In addition, through chat programs and videoconferencing, students can see each other online, share their ideas, and exchange knowledge (Beckman, 1999; Schofield, 1995). According to Berge and Collins (1995), Internet communication through e-mail and electronic discussion incorporates different learning styles, encourages and motivates learners, and allows learners to participate in the learning process individually. On a cautionary note, this kind of unlimited information requires learners to be selective and pedagogically trained in order to benefit from the resources in an efficient way. As Wood (1999)

17

asserts, there is a lack of advice on how to use the Internet for educational purposes. Thus, teachers should teach their learners how to take advantage of Internet sources in order to get its maximum benefits for language learning purposes.

Recently, there is a new trend in language teaching and learning: the use of podcasts. A podcast is a media file that is distributed over the Internet for playback on personal computers (PCs) and portable media players (Copley, 2007). The term 'podcasting' derives from Apple's iPod portable music player and was first proposed by journalist Ben Hammersley to describe listening to audio files on a portable media player (Hammersley, 2004). Podcasting can be described as creating content (audio or video) for people who want to listen, when they want, where they want, and how they want. A podcast might be on any topic so it is possible for learners to choose and download the files according to their interest. They are available for all levels of learners, so learners can select from archives according to their levels. Because podcasts serve as self-study materials, they are quite suitable for highly motivated or autonomous learners. One of the main advantages of podcasts is that they are easy to use and often available free on the Internet (Boulos, Maged, Maramba, Wheeler, 2006). Furthermore, podcasts can be produced by learners and teachers as well. Many teachers and professors prefer to record their lectures as podcasts so that students who have missed the class can download them to their computers and listen to them later. This is another advantage for the learners to catch up with the class (Dudeney & Hockly, 2007).

Advantages of CALL for Teachers

The literature on CALL also notes some advantages for teachers. These include being able to use class time in a more efficient way, making the teaching process easier and more flexible, enabling teachers to develop themselves professionally, offering the opportunity to monitor learners more easily, and providing the opportunity to find numerous resources for teaching.

Firstly, using computers can make it easier to save time in class and gives the opportunity to create materials in advance (Chapelle, 2001), so that students do not spend time waiting for the teacher to write on the board. Chapelle (2001) points out that computers can be used for corrections and marking exercises, which are mechanical tasks, so the teacher has more time to spend with the students for other activities. In addition, Chapelle (2001) states that if computers are used for language testing, teachers can save more time because computers do all the evaluation and calculation. Although the teacher might spend more time for the preparation of materials before the lessons, time spent during the lesson is used more efficiently by allowing students to ask more questions or practice the language since the materials are ready.

18

Secondly, more and more software programs are being produced by publishers nowadays, which may make the teaching process easier and more creative. For instance, teachers sometimes face difficulty in finding authentic materials for listening and speaking activities (Celce-Murcia, 2001). Today, there is a wide selection of activities and materials both on the Internet and in software programs, through which some subjects in grammar or a certain skill can be taught easily and effectively (Dudeney & Hockly, 2007). Since some of the materials are ready to be used instantly, the teacher's job is only finding and selecting them for the class. These materials can then enrich the teaching process and make it possible for the learners to learn the same topics from a variety of sources.

Finally, the Internet provides a wide range of resources for teachers to develop their teaching skills (Dudeney & Hockly, 2007). For instance, the use of blogs in writing classes or podcasts for listening comprehension activities is relatively new in classrooms. A teacher can find audio files permitted for downloading and ask his/her students to select and listen to those files regularly or ask the student to send their work to the blog for editing and grading. With the help of Internet-based resources, teachers can easily enhance their classes' productivity, authenticity, and enjoyment (May, 2005). The Internet and software programs can bring real life to the classroom by offering daily life speech samples for listening classes and sample audio and video files for authentic usage of language. In this way, the teacher not only makes the classes more enjoyable and attractive, but also guides the learners in benefitting from these sources in their free time.

Disadvantages of using CALL

In addition to the many advantages of using computers for educational purposes, there are some disadvantages of using CALL as well. These disadvantages are fewer than the advantages stated in different studies and reports in the literature, but they should also be considered while teaching and learning with computers.

First of all, computers should be thought of as a facilitator and a complement to the teaching and learning process. It is impossible for a computer to replace a teacher because a computer is dependent on the teacher. It is teachers who create and/or select educational materials, and control and load the necessary software and information (Ahmad et al., 1985). Teachers should not expect too much from computers since their capabilities are limited to their hardware and software. For instance, a computer cannot conduct an open-ended dialog with a student, whereas it is possible for two people to interact however they like.

Second, computers are not suitable for some of the activities or skill-based teaching in a classroom (Kenning & Kenning, 1983). For instance, after the 1990s, a great many software

19

programs were produced in order to facilitate learning, but most of them were prepared for individual use or computer laboratories, not the actual classroom. These software programs are best for reading, grammar, and listening because they can check learners' errors and give immediate feedback. However, as speaking and writing skills are productive skills, it is difficult for computers to assess such work, and software can only give limited feedback. Moreover, the interaction between computer and learner may not be the same as the way a teacher speaks to a student since the teacher has particular pedagogical aims and purposes in mind during this communication (Kenning & Kenning, 1983; Pennington, 1996). For instance, a teacher may give implicit error correction feedback by repeating what a student said and may wait for the student to correct himself/herself, whereas a computer either shows the correct answer or indicates that there is something wrong with that sentence by underlining it.

Third, teachers and learners need to have basic technology knowledge before starting to use computer technology in teaching and learning settings (Lai & Kritsonis, 2006). If learners are not competent enough to use computers, neither learners nor teachers can fully benefit from computerized-learning and teaching facilities. Although the age that one gains computer literacy is becoming lower day by day, there are still many students and teachers who cannot use a computer properly. In this case, computer-based activities and computer laboratory studies may not be easy for or applicable to some students. Using a keyboard, for instance, may not seem interesting or easy for some students and they may want a more traditional way of writing and reading.

Fourth, it is not possible to see the behavior of a human being in a computer. According to Howie (1989), computers lack these characteristics: ability to consider different personalities, ability to guess, and personal values. Thus, a teacher may guess what his/her student wants to say and help him/her. Teachers can adapt their techniques according to their students' individual differences so that every student may learn something from the lesson. On the other hand, computers cannot handle unexpected questions and responses. Since computers' artificial intelligence is limited, no one can expect computers to react or respond as human beings do (Lai & Kritsonis, 2006). Thus, a machine cannot substitute for a human being in an education process where interaction plays a key role; it may only be a facilitator and a supplementary tool for different kinds of activities.

Lastly, computer technology is not cheap to install in every school nor is it possible for every student to purchase a computer. As is stated in Lai and Kritsonis's (2006) article, for instance, if a school wants to equip all its classrooms with computers, the cost of education will increase and some schools will not be able to deal with this cost. In some institutions, two or three students have to share one computer because the institutions cannot afford one computer per one student. In this case, it is difficult to teach something to the entire class at the same time. Other options may result in scheduling issues about the use of computers among students (Criss, 2006). Moreover, software programs are not cheap enough for all institutions and students to purchase and benefit from those programs. Although technology as a whole is becoming cheaper, it is not cheap enough for all institutions, students, and parents to purchase and incorporate computer technologies in education.

Use of Interactive Whiteboards

So far, literature on CALL and its related issues were discussed. In this section, definition of an IWB, ways of IWB use in English classes, benefits and drawbacks of this technology, and attitudes of students and teachers towards IWB use will be discussed.

Definition and Requirements

The British Educational Communications and Technology Agency (BECTA) defines IWBs as follows:

> An interactive whiteboard is a large, touch-sensitive board which is connected to a digital projector and a computer. The projector displays the image from the computer screen on the board. The computer can then be controlled by touching the board, either directly or with a special pen. The potential applications are: using web-based resources in whole-class teaching, showing video clips to help explain concepts, presenting students' work to the rest of the classroom, creating digital flipcharts, manipulating text and practicing handwriting, and saving notes on the board for future use (BECTA, 2003b, p. 1).

The difference between an interactive whiteboard and a traditional whiteboard is that the teacher uses a special pen or his/her finger to manipulate images and texts on the whiteboard itself. The teacher can make annotations, compose original documents, bring students' documents onto the screen and edit them, get extra resources from the Internet, and allow the students to use them individually (Bell, 2002; Dudeney & Hockly, 2007).

There are three types of interactive whiteboards (Harris, 2005). The first type consists of an infrared/ultrasound kit that can be fixed to an existing traditional whiteboard. This system does not have the same nunber of functions as an active whiteboard. The second type is a passive whiteboard that is sensitive to finger manipulations and has more functions than an infrared kit. The last one is the active whiteboard, which can be used with both a special pen and a human finger. This kind of interactive whiteboard has the most functions (Harris, 2005). Interactive whiteboards are available in two forms: front projection and rear projection (Summet, Abowd, Corso, Rehg, 2005). Front-

21

projection interactive whiteboards have a video projector in front of the whiteboard. The disadvantage of these IWBs is that the presenter must stand in front of the screen and his/her body will cast a shadow. In contrast, rear-projection interactive whiteboards have the projector behind the whiteboard so that no shadows occur. Rear-projection boards are also advantageous because the presenter does not have to look into the projector light while speaking to the audience. The disadvantages of these systems are that they are generally more expensive than front-projection boards, are often large, and cannot be mounted flush on a wall (Summet et al., 2005).

There are also some other optional features of IWBs. Interactive whiteboards come in different sizes, but the most common one is 190 centimeters in width. The size of the board is important because students at the back of the classroom should be able to see the images and texts clearly (Smith, 2001). Another important point is about visibility. If sunlight shines directly onto the board, students cannot see the images clearly, and thus sun blinds should be used to cover the windows (Levy, 2002). In addition, a whiteboard can be portable or fixed, but if it is mobile, it has to be set up again each time when it is carried to another place. Among standard versions of IWBs, a backlit interactive whiteboard, which does not need a projector, is the most expensive kind of board (SDS, 2008).

Some important concerns should also be taken into consideration about the position of the board. The board should be mounted at a suitable height and the computer and projector should be positioned to minimise the risk posed by trailing wires (Smith, 2001). In primary schools, IWBs should be mounted at the right height so that young students, who are naturally smaller than adults, can write on them easily (Tameside MBC, 2003).

Ways of Using IWBs in English Classes

In English classes, IWBs are often used to support students in generating and amending text (Kennewell & Beauchamp, 2007). Using Microsoft Word, students can write their text on tablet PCs and that work can be displayed on the IWB and then the teacher can ask for editing suggestions to improve the paper. In this way, good papers can be rewarded and students may find the opportunity to compare their work with their peers' work on the IWB (Gerard, 1999). The teacher can also overwrite, underline, highlight, or circle any ill-formed elements in the text. In addition, a teacher can bring some pictures or a topic from the Internet that can be discussed by the students or used for the students' own presentations. Moreover, English teachers can take advantage of a variety of interactive games to practice new structures and words (Gray et al., 2005). Many pupils in Wall et al.'s (2005) study felt generally very positive about the use of games in lessons and they stated that IWBs make learning fun and easier. Language teachers can also benefit from the dictionaries and encyclopedias provided by either websites or software programs. If a student has a problem with a new word, the teacher can immediately display that word with all the forms and sample sentences. In this case, the students get a full picture of that word's use and its related structures. Furthermore, PowerPoint presentations can be useful and enjoyable for introducing new topics and they can be enhanced with other internet resources, audio, and visual items (Gray et al., 2005). In order to clarify abstract points of a subject, PowerPoint slides can be helpful to visualize those points and may attract the students' attention better than traditional ways of writing or explaining them on regular boards. Lastly, the teacher can benefit from the quizzes and tests included in software programs by employing them immediately with the students (Gerard, 1999).

Benefits of Interactive Whiteboards

Most of the literature on IWBs consists of highly positive perceptions about the impact and the potential of this technology. The benefits of IWB technology can be categorized into benefits for the students, and benefits for the teachers.

Benefits of IWBs for Students

Interactive whiteboards seem to offer several benefits for students. IWBs have been argued to increase student enjoyment and motivation (Levy, 2002; Schmid, 2006) and reduce the need for note-taking through the capacity to save and print what appears on the board (Bell, 2002; Walker, 2002). They may also make it possible to use resources flexibly and spontaneously for different needs of students (Levy, 2002; Walker, 2002) and increase the degree of understanding with the help of audio-visual materials (Bell, 2002; Gray et al., 2005; Hall & Higgins, 2005; Levy, 2002; Martin, 2007). Furthermore, IWBs have been shown to provide a greater number and wider variety of resources for learners (Hall & Higgins, 2005; Levy, 2002; Smith et al., 2005), enable learners to be more creative in their presentations in the classrooms (Bell, 2002; Levy, 2002), and provide opportunities for students' participation and collaboration in the classroom (Gray et al., 2005; Levy, 2002; Schmid, 2007).

Levy (2002) conducted a small-scale study of the use of IWBs at two secondary schools in England. He interviewed 11 teachers and distributed questionnaires to 286 students and collected a great deal of data showing the teachers' and students' perceptions of IWB use. According to the students' responses, IWBs make lessons more enjoyable, entertaining, and fun, and the students are more interested in the lessons because teachers' explanations are clearer. In addition, multimedia resources and the IWB's large screen help the students understand easily, which also contributes to increasing their motivation. Some of the teachers also pointed out that children are more attentive because they are curious about what will come up next. Furthermore, in a study conducted by Wall,

① 2 secondary schools;²³ "IWBs make lessons more fun"
— watch videos?? Better engaging activities? . . ?

Higgins, and Smith (2005), which investigated the views of primary school students towards IWBs, some students responded that they would be very happy to have their work shown on the IWB and they had a strong desire to use the IWB individually, which might help them be more engaged in the lesson.

Bell (2002) notes that IWBs allow for the students' work to be copied, printed, and then distributed to the whole class. In this way, for instance, a relatively well-written composition can be used as a sample for the other students, or the teacher can choose the work of one of the students' and distribute it to the rest of the class members so that they can work on finding the mistakes or giving suggestions to improve it. Another alternative is that after a brainstorming activity, the document on which the ideas are written can be printed and distributed to the class and the teacher can assign homework using those ideas to write an essay.

In Levy's study (2002), teachers reported that IWB resources could be used flexibly according to the immediate needs of the students. For instance, using the palette, made up of some icons and shapes, on the side of the IWB screen makes it possible for the teacher to go forward and backward depending on the needs of the .learners. It is also possible to show previous materials if some of the students were unable to understand the topic clearly or missed the class. Another opportunity for the teacher is to change the pace of the lesson. If the students are slow to learn new subjects, the teacher can incorporate more materials to prompt the students to understand the new item or if the case is just the opposite, the teacher may provide more advanced materials for the quick learners. Walker (2002) also praises this facility, adding that IWBs can be suitable for on-the-spot changes during the lessons and give teachers more freedom to decide what to do next according to the new situation.

Several studies have reported that, thanks to the audio and visual materials associated with IWBs, students can easily understand even abstract concepts, and using images and audio files promotes effective learning (Bell, 2002; Gray et al., 2005; Hall & Higgins, 2005; Martin, 2007; Wall et al. 2005). According to a study done by Martin (2007), a high percentage of children agreed that the pictures and the sound help them to understand better. In Wall et al.'s (2005) study, the children pointed out that the pictures help them to understand what the teacher is talking about. In another study conducted by Hall and Higgins (2005), primary school students were interviewed regarding their perceptions of the use of IWBs. Almost all the students stated that they most enjoyed the multi-media capabilities including the audio and visual aspects, and the opportunity to touch the board. Futhermore, Bell (2002) points out that IWBs can provide materials for different learning styles such as tactile, audio, and visual. With the help of the variety of the materials, different types of learners in a classroom can benefit from this technology.

24

Hall and Higgins (2005), Levy (2002), and Smith et al. (2005) support the notion that IWBs are versatile devices and can provide a wide variety of resources from which the learners can benefit. For instance, Levy (2002), relying on a teacher's report, points out that for each lesson, different materials can be used, such as sound, video, and images, which may prevent boredom and hold the students' attention as long as possible. Both Smith et al. (2005) and Hall and Higgins (2005) maintain that the Internet and other peripherals enable students to reach a wide range of resources, including games and some software facilities as well. They also note that IWBs are suitable for all ages, but generally IWBs are most liked by younger learners because they seem to appreciate the touch sensitive feature of IWBs and the opportunity to play games with IWBs.

According to Gray et al. (2005), Levy (2002), and Schmid (2007), interactive whiteboards provide more opportunities for students to participate in the lesson and collaborate with their classmates. Some of the teachers in Gray et al.'s (2005) study stated that the use of IWBs enhances pupil participation when compared to paper-based activities. Students in Levy's (2002) study reported that IWBs are powerful devices which, due to their large screen size, hold the class together and stimulate participation across the class as a whole.

Benefits of IWBs for Teachers

Research has also noted benefits that IWBs provide for teachers. Using IWB-based resources may reduce time spent in writing and leave more time for teaching (Levy, 2002), and materials generated in the classroom can be saved, printed, and re-used later (Levy, 2002; Walker, 2002). In addition, teachers have pointed out that they are more inventive, creative, and effective in their explanations when they use IWBs (Levy, 2002; Wall et al., 2005). Furthermore, since teachers can provide immediate feedback to the learners and incorporate more samples (Cuthell, 2005), IWBs may increase the pace of teaching and give an opportunity to the teachers to be more flexible (Kennewell, 2001; Moss et al., 2007). IWBs have also been argued to make it easier for teachers to keep the class together, keep the students' attention longer, and motivate students (Kennewell & Beauchamp, 2007; Smith, 1999).

Levy (2002) states that when the teachers use materials prepared before class, they save time for other teaching activities. With IWBs, teachers can allocate more time for the students, focusing on individual problems, extra challenging tasks, and communicative activities, because they do not spend a lot of time writing on the board. Normally, when the teacher is writing on the board, he/she is facing the board not the class, so the teacher might not keep control over the class.

In Wall et al.'s (2005) study, which was conducted with 80 students at 12 English primary schools, pupils commented that they felt their teacher was more inventive and active during the

25

[Handwritten note at top:] Qn is: Does IWB make teachers more inventive & creative?

IWB-based class. The teacher seemed better able to find original ideas or interesting ways to teach the subjects in a fun way. Because of this, the students were no longer bored. Levy (2002) also mentions reports of teachers' being considered more effective with their explanations because IWBs have many visual materials and vivid illustrations. Her participants felt IWBs made the teaching process more interesting, interactive, and exciting.

Another benefit of IWBs noted in some studies is that they increase the pace of teaching and give the opportunity to teachers to be more flexible (Kennewell, 2001; Moss et al., 2007). According to Kennewell (2001), a wide range of internet resources made accessible by the IWB allows the teacher to choose materials flexibly in order to cover the diverse needs and consider the different characteristics of the students in a classroom. In addition, Moss et al. (2007) point out that the pace of teaching can be increased by bringing in and moving between the texts or materials quickly. When learner characteristics are taken into consideration, it was shown that for students who are quick and good at learning new items, the pace of the lesson can be increased and the lesson can be made more challenging with extra materials. *[Handwritten: Very vague... boils down to: You can show lots of materials quickly.]*

Drawbacks and Difficulties of Interactive Whiteboards

Although the benefits of IWBs in the literature outnumber the drawbacks, studies have also shown that there are some important difficulties and drawbacks which may hinder the expansion of this technology. The lack of teachers' confidence and competence in using IWBs (Glover & Miller, 2001; Hall & Higgins, 2005; Levy, 2002; Wall et al., 2005), extra time needed for the planning and preparation of the materials (Gray et al., 2005; Levy, 2002), the need for special training (Gray et al., 2005; Hall & Higgins, 2005; Levy, 2002; Moss et al., 2007), and technical issues such as the possibility of breaking down, the need for recalibration, and position of the board (Hall & Higgins, 2005; Levy, 2002; Wall et al., 2005) are the main problems or difficulties that both students and teachers face while using this technology.

In Levy's (2002), Hall and Higgins's (2005), and Wall et al.'s (2005) studies, some pupils reported that the lack of teachers' competence in using IWBs causes problems during the lessons. For instance, if the teacher is not comfortable with finding necessary files, the students get bored and the real value of this technology is not understood. This kind of competence includes both technical and pedagogical aspects of IWB use. In other words, the teacher should know how to benefit from IWBs both in terms of teaching techniques and flexibility of using the resources for the different needs of students. According to Levy (2002), teachers who have confidence in ICT are more comfortable with the use of IWBs. This finding demonstrates that teachers should receive training to integrate ICT and IWB technology into classroom settings.

In line with this, many studies indicate that there is a need for training in order to take advantage of IWB technology fully. Levy (2002) states that teachers who have no or little knowledge of ICT should receive special training in the use of IWBs individually, in particular, because some teachers may have barriers regarding the use of technology and need more time and practice to be confident in using the technology in class. Hall and Higgins (2005) point out that teachers should be trained to learn not only technical but also pedagogical aspects of IWB technology and this training should be continuous. In addition, Moss et al. (2007) and Gray et al. (2005) stress the importance of training to help teachers understand the real value of IWBs for teaching and learning and the role of training for personal development in order to be more effective and creative teachers.

Both Gray et al. (2005) and Levy (2002) reveal that teachers need more time to prepare resources and plan IWB-based lessons. Teachers cannot use their traditionally prepared materials for IWB-installed classrooms. They have to plan when to display extra materials, how to design the activities so that more interaction can take place in the class with the help of the IWB, and determine what kind of activities to use to enhance the learning process. They also have to plan the amount of time they will allocate for the actual use of the IWB during the class time, because some students may find it boring when IWBs are overused (Levy, 2002).

Since this technology is more complicated compared to traditional blackboards or overhead projectors (OHP), technical problems may occur more often. In Levy (2002), students reported that half of the time IWBs do not work properly and sometimes if they break down, the teacher may not have anything to use for rest of the class time. Some students also complained about the difficulty of using the electronic pen and noted problems related to the manipulation of the images on the board. In Hall and Higgins (2005), some students reported the problem of freezing, which means the teacher has to switch the IWB off and on again. In this case, the teacher has to reload everything, which wastes time. In addition, if the IWB does not display the images and texts properly, it needs recalibration and this process has to be repeated each time if the place of the whiteboard is changed. Lastly, the positioning of the IWB is also very important (Smith, 2001). Especially for young students it is easier to touch and write on the board if the IWB is mounted at a suitable height.

According to Gray et al. (2005), use of the IWB in conjunction with PowerPoint can lead teachers to a "show and tell" style of teaching, which pushes students to be more passive. In their study, one of the teachers stated that the IWB changed the teachers' role, making them less involved in the teaching process because they only deliver the material for the students with the help of the IWB. This in turn may cause a decline in the authority of the teacher in the classroom. Another

27

This contradicts the plus comment that teachers are more inventive & flexible, and students more involved/moti point about the use of IWBs is that there are different types of interactivity when IWBs are used in the lessons. The interaction can be between pupils and pupils, teachers and pupils, and IWBs and pupils (Birmingham, Davies & Greiffenhagen, 2002). If IWBs are not used as tools for enhancing the interaction between pupils and IWBs in a proper way, the teacher's role in the classroom can be questioned by the students. Another study (Gray et al., 2007) indicates that due to the increase in the pace of the lesson through the quick manipulation of images, the result may be limited interaction between the teacher and the students. Furthermore, according to Goodison (2003), teachers are cautious that their lessons may become more teacher-centered if too much focus is given to the IWB technology. They caution that there must be a balance between the use of IWBs and traditional teaching activities and techniques, which give more opportunity to the teachers to take responsibility for the teaching process.

As it is expensive to invest in computer technology, educators have to reconsider their priorities and budgets. Harris (2005) points out that IWB technology is not cheap, for instance, the least expensive IWB costs approximately £1500 (3750 YTL). Not all schools can afford this technology investment without a government policy and some kind of funding. However, infrared kits are the cheapest kind of IWB technology, providing many basic functions of IWBs, so for a start these kits may be a short-term solution to access this technology.

Attitudes of Students and Teachers towards the Use of Interactive Whiteboards

In the literature on IWBs, some studies have focused particularly on the attitudes and views of students (Hall & Higgins, 2005; Kennewell & Morgan, 2003; Wall et al., 2005). Other studies have investigated the perceptions of both teachers and students (Beeland, 2002; Glover & Miller, 2001; Levy, 2002; Moss et al., 2007; Schmid, 2006), and one study examined the opinions of only teachers (Lee & Boyle, 2004). Overall, both students and teachers are positive about the use of IWBs in their lessons and appreciate the benefits of IWBs.

The studies conducted by Moss et al. (2007), Wall et al. (2005), and Hall and Higgins (2005) revealed students' perceptions of the use of IWBs in different subject areas (e.g. math, science). The findings in those studies showed that the majority of the students have positive opinions about IWB use in the lessons. The findings also indicated that the students appreciated the versatility of IWB technology, and its ability to incorporate a wide variety of resources, and they pointed out that IWBs added some value to the lessons. Moss et al. (2007) and Glover and Miller (2001) also found that students were positive about the contributions of IWBs to learning in terms of making difficult things easier to understand and increasing motivation.

28

or audio tapes!

With regard to teachers' attitudes, Smith (1999), Moss et al. (2007), Glover and Miller (2001), and Lee and Boyle (2004) contributed to the literature on IWBs reporting the attitudes of teachers about IWBs. In general, the teachers reported their positive attitudes in these studies and were impressed by the functions of IWBs. According to the teachers' comments in these studies, IWBs are effective tools in enhancing student learning and help their lessons to be more enjoyable, interesting, and motivating. *But what's the difference? IWBs or computer / projector? (or even one!)*

Although these various studies have investigated the attitudes of students or teachers, only Schmid (2006) and Gray et al. (2005) focused on students' and/or teachers' attitudes in language learning settings. Schmid (2006) conducted a small-scale qualitative study, in which he collected data from a small group of students who were taking an English for Academic Purposes course in Lancaster University. The aim of the study was to obtain an understanding of the processes and analyze the use of IWBs from the perspective of a critical theory of technology. The findings showed that several elements, such as the inherent charcteristics of the technology, pedagogical beliefs, and students' own understanding affect technology use in a certain context. Gray et al. (2005) is a case study of twelve English teachers in Britain. While it provides information about the language teachers' positive opinions about the potential of IWB technology, giving some suggestions for the effective use of this technology as well, it fails to provide a broad and comprehensive understanding of language teachers' views about the use of IWBs in language teaching. In short, there remains a need for a larger-scale study, focusing on language instruction contexts, and including all stakeholders.

Conclusion

This chapter presented the relevant literature about CALL and IWBs. The use of IWBs in education dates back to the late 1990s in some developed countries, but in technologically developing countries, such as Turkey, they are now becoming more common in educational institutions. IWB technology offers a great many benefits; however, it is important to note that there needs to be adequate training and a careful selection of relevant materials in order to take advantage of the full functions of this technology (Harris, 2005). As for the literature on CALL and IWB technology, students and teachers have, in general, positive opinions and are aware of the benefits of technology in education. However, it takes time to incorporate new technologies in education due to factors such as financial barriers, training of users, misconceptions about technology and computers, and availability of adequate and good materials (Lee, 2000). While computers will not become substitute for teachers, they will continue to be useful supplementary tools in education well into the future. The next chapter will present the methodology used in this study, including participants and setting, instruments, procedure, and data analysis.

29

CHAPTER III: METHODOLOGY

Introduction

This study investigated attitudes of students and teachers towards the use of interactive whiteboards in EFL classrooms. The study specifically examined how English teachers and EFL students perceive IWB technology and how they benefit from this technology. The study also aimed to learn administrators' perceptions of this technology and the ways that English teachers use the technology in language classes.

The study addressed the following questions:

1) What are the attitudes of Turkish EFL teachers towards interactive whiteboards?

2) What are the attitudes of Turkish EFL students towards interactive whiteboards?

3) What are the attitudes of administrators in Turkish educational contexts towards interactive whiteboards?

4) How are IWBs used in EFL classrooms in Turkey?

5) What factors may influence Turkish students' and teachers' attitudes towards the use of IWBs in EFL classrooms?

This chapter presents the setting and participants of the study, the instruments used for data collection, the procedures of data collection, and data analysis.

Participants and Setting

Since this study was limited by the number of educational institutions in Turkey that use IWB technology, there could not be equal distribution of the types of institutions. This study was conducted, therefore, in thirteen different educational institutions where IWB technology is used in Turkey. Some of the students who participated in the study were preparatory class students in universities and high schools, others were in language schools taking English courses at different levels, and others were primary school students taking English classes at least two days a week. In any one institution, not all classrooms using IWBs in English classes were necessarily surveyed. In any institution, if there were more than three classrooms where IWBs were installed, the three classes in which IWB had been used most often were surveyed.

If the students' IWB exposure was the same, one sample from each grade and level was chosen at random. The age of students ranged from 6 to mid-40s since there were educational institutions ranging from primary school to language school. The highest student population in this survey belongs to university students (45%) (see Table 1).

Table 1: Background information of students

Age			Gender			Institution		
Age	f	%		f	%		f	%
6-14	179	39.08	Male	270	58.95	Primary school	178	38.86
15-19	175	38.21	Female	188	41.05	Secondary school	71	15.50
20-25	93	20.31				University	204	44.54
25+	11	2.40				Language school	5	1.09
Total	458	100.00	Total	458	100.00	Total	458	100.00
State/Private			Hours of IWB Exposure			English Level		
	f	%		f	%		f	%
State	206	44.98	1-2 hours*	156	34.06	Elementary	82	17.90
Private	252	55.02	3-5 hours*	114	24.89	Pre-Intermediate	173	37.77
			6-10 hours*	116	25.33	Intermediate	147	32.10
			10+ hours*	72	15.72	Upper-		
			* a week			Intermediate	46	10.04
						Advanced	10	2.18
Total	458	100.00	Total	458	100.00	Total	458	100.00

Note: f: Frequency, %: percentage

The teachers surveyed also came from these thirteen different educational institutions, and therefore ranged from primary school teachers to university instructors. They had varying degrees of experience in teaching English, with the majority (83%) having between 1-10 years experience (see Table 2). Among all English teachers in any institution, only the ones with actual experience using this technology were involved in the survey. In order to see the actual use of IWBs in English classes, three hours of English lessons were observed. Two of these classes were observed in one university, and the other was observed in a secondary school. The criterion for choosing the lesson to be observed was the amount of the teacher's experience in using this technology. Lastly, three administrators were interviewed to investigate their attitudes towards the use of IWBs. All administrators were from universities and they were chosen because they had either had enough knowledge about IWB technology or had participated in the decision-making process to purchase the IWB technology.

Table 2: Background information of teachers

Age	f	%	Years of Experience	f	%	Institution	f	%
20-25	18	21.95	1-5 years	42	51.22	Primary school	16	19.51
26-30	34	41.46	6-10 years	27	32.93	High school	9	10.98
31-35	17	20.73	11-15 years	4	4.88	University	44	53.66
36-40	4	4.88	16-20 years	5	6.10	Language school	13	15.85
41-45	5	6.10	21+ years	4	4.88			
46+	4	4.88						
Total	82	100.00	Total	82	100.00	Total	82	100.00

Gender	f	%	Hours of IWB use	f	%	State/Private Institution	f	%
Male	12	14.63	1-2 hours*	22	26.83	State	18	21.95
Female	70	85.37	3-5 hours*	14	17.07	Private	64	78.05
			6-10 hours*	8	9.76			
			11+ hours*	38	46.34			
			* a week					
Total	82	100.00	Total	82	100.00	Total	82	100.00

Note: f: Frequency, %: percentage

Instruments

Survey techniques and instruments were used in order to collect data in this study. Two questionnaires were employed in this study in order to collect data about the attitudes of students and teachers towards IWBs in language teaching and learning settings. Both the student and teacher questionnaires included five point Likert-scale items, open-ended and multiple-choice items, and apart from primary and secondary school students, the rest of the participants signed a consent form (see Appendix A). The first questionnaire elicited information about the attitudes of students towards IWB use in English lessons (see Appendix B). The other questionnaire explored the attitudes of EFL teachers towards IWB use in the classroom settings (see Appendix C). While writing the questions in the questionnaire, the researcher was inspired by Moss et al's (2007) questionnaire on teacher and student perceptions of IWBs in core subjects (e.g. math and science). Some teacher and student responses in Levy's (2000) study were also used to prepare the questionnaire items for this study. After the writing of the final version of the student's questionnaire in English, the questions in the student's questionnaire were translated into Turkish by the researcher and checked by a fellow English teacher, in case student participants would not understand some of the statements in English. However, the teacher's questionnaire was written in English because it was felt that EFL teachers would easily understand the questionnaire items. In order to improve the questionnaires, a pilot study was conducted in Middle East Technical University's Foreign Languages Department. Forty students and five teachers participated in the study in total. After the study, two vague items in the teacher's questionnaire were changed in order to be clearer. The reliability check with Cronbach Alpha resulted in the score of 0,79 for student's questionnaire and 0.78 for teacher's questionnaire. In the teacher's questionnaire, three opposite items were excluded before the reliability check.

In order to explore the attitudes of administrators towards the use of IWBs, an interview protocol was used (see Appendix D). I conducted these interviews with the heads of the Foreign Languages Departments in three different universities. They were the administrators of the preparatory programs. The reason for including administrators in this study is that their attitudes are also important while deciding to purchase this technology and provide additional support for teachers. There were six questions in total, exploring the factors influencing their institutions' decision to purchase IWBs, their opinions about the benefits of IWBs, the most common problems stated by the EFL teachers, and general background information about the institution. The interviews were held in Turkish, and after the recording of the participants' speeches on a voice recorder, the researcher transcribed those speeches and translated them into English. The data were analyzed in terms of positive or negative attitudes towards the use of IWBs in language instruction.

For the last research question, a video recording procedure was conducted. The purpose of this procedure was to observe the actual ways in which of EFL teachers used or benefited from IWBs in language classes. In this way, there could be an opportunity to compare the use of IWBs as stated in the literature and in other countries with EFL teachers' use of IWBs in Turkey.

Procedure

In January 2008, with the help of publishers and IWB technology marketing firms, the Turkish educational institutions that possess IWB technology were identified. It was learned that approximately seventy different institutions possess this technology, but only about twenty of them use it in language classes. I phoned the administrations of the institutions that use IWB in language classes to learn whether they actually use this technology or not. I found out that even though some of these institutions had purchased IWBs, they were not using them actively, maybe due to the need for training. Some of the institutions requested official permission from the director of education in different cities, so I excluded those institutions from my list since it would take a long time to get that permission. At the end of this initial searching step, I made a list of fifteen institutions that use IWBs in EFL classrooms, and which consented to take part in this study. Two of the institutions ultimately did not send back the questionnaires, leaving a total of thirteen institutions surveyed. The return rate, in this case, is approximately 80% with student's questionnaire and 19% with teacher's questionnaire.

In order to conduct this study, an official letter requesting the necessary permission for data collection was sent in February to the administration of the four institutions that requested an official letter. The head of the Foreign Languages department or the committee in one of the universities sent back letters that indicated their approval of the request. The other institutions consented to participate in this study without requesting an official letter. The pilot study was held in the METU preparatory school. Forty students and five teachers participated in the piloting procedure. A preparatory classroom was selected randomly, taking into consideration that they had some degree of IWB use experience. Two teachers who had been using this technology for one year were selected for the piloting. The student questionnaires were distributed to the EFL students in the preparatory class and all the students completed the questionnaires. The other questionnaire, which was designed for the teachers who use IWBs in English classes, was distributed to the teachers and five teachers completed this questionnaire. The researcher requested the students and the teachers to comment on unclear statements and to express their thoughts about the questions and the survey itself. The time spent for each questionnaire was also recorded. After the piloting, minor changes to improve the questionnaires were made with the help of the teachers' oral and written comments and the students' feedback.

After the minor changes in the questionnaires were made, the questionnaires were distributed to fifteen institutions by post. Three interviews were then held with the heads of three institutions. Six questions were asked to learn their beliefs about this technology. Three hours of English classes were recorded in different institutions, using a digital video camera. After the recording, the tapes were analyzed using a checklist to define the ways in which English teachers used this technology. The checklist, which was compiled on the basis of uses mentioned in the literature on IWBs, consisted of different activities and ways of IWB use, such as bringing in materials from the Internet (see Appendix F).

The study was conducted during the first three weeks of March by distributing the questionnaires to the institutions. The researcher visited most of the institutions and collected the data himself. Four of the institutions were far from Ankara and Istanbul, thus the questionnaires were sent to these institutions and returned by post. The interviews were conducted in the second week of April 2008 and the observations of the English classes were completed the following week.

Data analysis

All the items in the questionnaires were analyzed using the Statistical Package for Social Sciences (SPSS), with the exception of the two open-ended questions at the end of both the teachers' questionnaire and students' questionnaire. In the interview with the administrators, there were six questions and they were analyzed through categorization of the responses in terms of positive and negative opinions. For every item statistically analyzed, frequencies and percentages were calculated. In terms of mean scores and standard deviations, the researcher excluded the option "No idea" from the variables in order to see only the degree of actual agreement and disagreement among the participants expressing a clear opinion. Therefore, the calculation of mean scores ranged from 1.00 to 4.00. In this case, the scores between 1.00 and 1.75 meant that the participants showed their strong disagreement with a certain statement, 1.76-2.50 indicated disagreement, 2.51-3.25 showed agreement, and 3.26-4.00 corresponded to strong agreement. In order to find whether there was a significant relation between different variables such as age, hours of IWB use/exposure and students' and teachers' having positive or negative attitudes towards IWBs, one-way ANOVA tests were performed. Interviews with the administrators were taped and transcribed by the researcher. The transcript data were categorized according to administrators' positive or negative attitudes towards the use of IWB technology. The video records were analyzed and categorized according to the ways that teachers use IWBs in the literature. In addition, the open-ended responses from the students were first translated into English, and then categorized according to the sections in the analysis of the questionnaire data gathered from the students. Later, after each section of the analysis of the student questionnaire results, the related responses were added to the relevant sections in order to support or contradict with the students' or teachers' Likert-scale responses.

Conclusion

This chapter gave the general information about the participants, the instruments used in the study, and the procedure followed during the study. In the next chapter, the data analysis and the findings will be discussed in detail.

CHAPTER IV: DATA ANALYSIS

Introduction

This study explored the attitudes of students and teachers towards the use of interactive whiteboards in language classrooms. Students and teachers at thirteen educational institutions were surveyed. Six of the institutions where the questionnaires were administered were private institutions and the rest were state institutions. The interviews, through which administrators' attitudes were explored, were conducted at three different educational institutions. Finally, in a state university and a private high school, a total of three hours of English classes were recorded by camcorder to see the actual use of interactive whiteboards.

The study aimed to provide information about how students and EFL teachers perceive the use of interactive whiteboards in English classes. The interviews held with the administrators elicited information about how heads of English departments and administrators of schools perceive the use of interactive whiteboards in language classes and to what extent they support the use of this technology.

This study addressed the following questions:

1) What are the attitudes of Turkish EFL teachers towards interactive whiteboards?

2) What are the attitudes of Turkish EFL students towards interactive whiteboards?

3) What are the attitudes of administrators in Turkish educational contexts towards interactive whiteboards?

4) How are IWBs used in EFL classrooms in Turkey?

5) What factors may influence Turkish students' and teachers' attitudes towards the use of IWBs in EFL classrooms?

Data Analysis Procedure

With the exception of section three, in which there were two open-ended response items, all sections in the questionnaires were analyzed statistically. The Statistical Packages for Social Sciences (SPSS) Version 11.5 was used to compute frequencies and percentages of each Likert-scale question. All the Likert-scale items consisted of a 5-point format: strongly agree, agree, no idea, disagree, and strongly disagree. While calculating means and standard deviations, the option "No idea" was excluded from the variables in order to see only the degree of actual agreement and disagreement among the participants. ANOVA tests were also calculated to see whether there was a significant relationship between attitudes and various participant factors, including age, years of teaching experience, hours of IWB exposure, and type of the institution worked in. In addition, responses from the two open-ended questions were grouped according to the similar questions in

36

the second section of the questionnaire and were discussed after each statistical analysis. The interview transcript data were analyzed according to the responses of interviewees for each of the six questions. The researcher examined all the responses for each question in order to find similarities and differences between the attitudes of the administrators. Finally, the observation data were analyzed in order to reflect the actual use of IWBs in English lessons and to what extent the potential of IWBs is exploited.

The results obtained from the analysis of the questionnaires are presented in four parts below. In the first part, the analysis of questions in the student questionnaire is presented according to six categories: learning, technical issues, affective factors, motivation, time/organization, and differences between IWBs and traditional whiteboards. In the second part, the responses given to the questions in the teacher's questionnaire are shown according to four categories: teaching, attitudes, motivation, and training. In the third part, the data gathered from the interviews are presented according to the six questions asked, and the similarities and differences between the interviewees' responses for each question addressing attitudes towards the use of IWBs are analyzed. The final part of this chapter is devoted to a presentation of the various ways of actual IWB use in English classes as seen during the class observations.

Part 1: Students' Attitudes towards the Use of Interactive Whiteboards

Section 1: Students' Attitudes Related to Learning

The questions in this section of the questionnaire aimed to investigate students' attitudes towards the use of IWBs in terms of their perceived effect on learning. This section was comprised of six questions in total, for all of which the students could show their degree of agreement or disagreement by circling options from 1 (strongly disagree) to 5 (strongly agree). The first question aimed to find out overall whether the students felt that they learn more when an IWB is used in English classes. The second question addressed whether lessons in which IWBs are used are easier to understand. The remaining questions were intended to learn whether the students felt IWBs made their teachers' drawings easier and clearer to see, whether using audio and visual materials with IWBs helped their understanding, whether IWBs allow them to learn from a wider range of sources, and in general, whether IWBs make learning more interesting.

Table 3: Student attitudes about IWBs and learning

		SD	D	NI	A	SA	Mean*
Q1	f	24	40	78	199	117	3.03
	%	5.24	8.73	17.03	43.45	25.55	
Q2	f	17	43	62	188	148	3.12
	%	3.71	9.39	13.54	41.05	32.31	
Q3	f	19	57	74	160	148	3.03
	%	4.15	12.45	16.16	34.93	32.31	
Q4	f	9	28	50	180	191	3.31
	%	1.97	6.11	10.92	39.30	41.70	
Q5	f	18	44	78	153	165	3.22
	%	3.93	9.61	17.03	33.41	36.03	
Q14	f	20	25	47	183	183	3.29
	%	4.37	5.46	10.26	39.96	39.96	

Note: f: Frequency SD: Strongly disagree D: Disagree NI: No idea A: Agree SA: Strongly agree STD: Standard Deviation

Mean*: Means calculated without the NI responses

Q1: I learn more when my teacher uses the interactive whiteboard in English classes.

Q2: It is easier to understand the lesson when my teacher uses an IWB.

Q3: IWBs make the teachers' drawings and diagrams easier to see.

Q4: Using audio and visual materials with IWBs helps me understand the language classes better.

Q5: I find the opportunity to learn from different sources with the use of IWBs.

Q14: IWBs make language learning more interesting and exciting.

By considering the mean scores, we can understand that the students agreed with all of the statements in this category. Regarding the responses for the fourth question, which has the highest mean score, it is seen that most of the students think that using audio and visual materials helps them to understand the lessons better. Showing these materials is easier with IWBs and the students can benefit from seeing them on a big screen, which seems to attract their attention. In general, a large majority (79%) of the participants agreed that IWB use in English classes makes the lessons more interesting and exciting (Q14). For the fifth question, a majority (69%) of the students agreed that IWBs make it possible to bring in and benefit from materials from different sources such as the Internet, students' own work, and other software programs. Table 3 also shows that the Mean scores of both Q1 and Q3 are the same (M=3.03) Two thirds of the students either agreed or strongly agreed that they learn more when an IWB is used in English lessons. Sixty-seven percent of the students agreed that IWBs help the teachers to draw clearer pictures and show their handwritten texts in Microsoft word format (Q3), but it is also seen that there is a considerable number of participants who have no idea about this issue. This might be because drawing and showing diagrams is more prevalent in math and science classes, and this opportunity may not be applied so much in English lessons.

By looking at the open-ended responses, thirty-seven participants wrote comments that might be relevant to this category. These comments were categorized as positive or negative. In terms of general positive responses, ten students simply requested the installment of IWBs into every classroom; using statements such as:

I want all the classrooms equipped with IWBs (Student 27).

Other students made more specific comments related to IWB use and learning. Three students pointed out that colors and visuals attract their attention so they learn a topic quickly. Four respondents also declared that IWBs help them learn better and IWBs ease learning. Moreover, one student stated that they have got rid of chalk dust and also have started to access the Internet during the lesson, which provides an opportunity to learn something from many other sources.

In terms of negative comments, ten of the respondents complained about the shortage of IWB-based lessons due to the fact that there is only one smart class at their schools, which is a negative comment, but with ultimately a positive implication for the use of IWBs. One student stated that not everyone could learn better when an IWB is used during the language classes. The student did not elaborate on this statement, but clearly felt strongly enough about it to write it down in the open-ended section. Six respondents took the opportunity to write in a general comment that they prefer traditional boards because they learn better with them. Interestingly, two of the students wrote only that they wanted IWBs to be removed from the classrooms.

Section 2: Students' Attitudes Related to Technical Issues

There were two questionnaire items aiming to explore the students' attitudes towards the use of IWBs specifically in terms of technical issues (see Table 4). The first question asked whether problems with the screen and sunlight make it hard for the students to see the texts or images on the IWB. The second question was about the problem of technical breakdowns and the resulting issue of wasting time for recalibration.

Table 4: Student's attitudes related to technical issues

		SD	D	NI	A	SA	Mean*
Q6	F	60	69	45	156	128	2.85
	%	13.10	15.07	9.83	34.06	27.95	
Q7	F	102	88	117	94	57	2.31
	%	22.27	19.21	25.55	20.52	12.45	

Note: f: Frequency SD: Strongly disagree D: Disagree NI: No idea A: Agree SA: Strongly agree STD: Standard Deviation

Mean*: Means calculated without the NI responses

Q6: Sometimes deficiencies of the IWB screen and sunlight in the classroom make it difficult to see the things on the IWB.

Q7: IWBs often break down and recalibration causes a waste of time.

The results in this section show that the majority of students agreed that the sunlight issue is an important one, whereas they disagreed with the notion that IWBs break down very often. As can be seen in Table 4, 62% of the students agreed that problems with sunlight and screens sometimes prevent them from seeing the images and texts on IWBs. For the seventh item, the students' ideas are a bit mixed. While a slightly larger group disagrees with the idea that frequent technical breakdowns ultimately make IWBs a waste of time, a considerable number of students do still agree with the same idea, and the largest single group (26%) report having no idea. This seems to indicate that the plurality of the students has not faced IWB breakdowns or if they have, that these problems were solved in a short time.

Seven of the students chose to particularly note that IWBs often break down and that both breakdowns and other technical problems cause a waste of time in the open-ended section of the questionnaire. Nearly a quarter of the forty students who wrote technical related comments in the open-ended section complained about the sunlight effect and requested that curtains be installed on the windows. One of the respondents indicated that it is not easy to use the IWB pencil and sometimes it does not work properly. Three participants complained about the warning that appears on the board saying that the filter needs cleaning, adding that this warning irritates them during the lesson. One student complained about the small size of the IWB screen, explaining that it is difficult for her to see.

Section 3: Students' Attitudes Related to Affective Factors

This section was composed of four questions related to the students' overall feelings and opinions about the use of IWBs in language classes (see Table 5). The first question was asked in order to explore their feelings about using IWBs in front of their classmates. The second question intended to investigate the students' opinions on the ease or difficulty of using IWBs. The next item directly addressed the students' preference for IWB-based lessons and the last question in this category aimed to learn whether the students feel uncomfortable when their work is shown on an IWB.

Table 5: Student's attitudes related to affective factors

		SD	D	NI	A	SA	Mean*
Q8	f	46	46	116	95	155	3.05
	%	10.04	10.04	25.33	20.74	33.84	
Q9	f	188	114	85	36	35	1.78
	%	41.05	24.89	18.56	7.86	7.64	
Q10	f	27	42	84	130	175	3.21
	%	5.90	9.17	18.34	28.38	38.21	
Q11	f	170	107	95	52	34	1.87
	%	37.12	23.36	20.74	11.35	7.42	

Note: f: Frequency SD: Strongly disagree D: Disagree NI: No idea A: Agree SA: Strongly agree STD: Standard Deviation

Mean*: Means calculated without the NI responses

Q8: I like going to the front of the class to use the IWB.

Q9: It seems difficult for me to use IWBs.

Q10: I prefer language classes that are taught with an IWB.

Q11: It makes me uncomfortable when my work is shown to the whole class on the IWB.

Looking at the results in Table 5, there is only a slight difference between the mean scores of the two "negative" questions (Q9, Q11), revealing that the students disagreed with the ideas that IWBs are difficult to use or that they feel uncomfortable having their work shown to the whole class. On the other hand, the students agreed with the statement about liking to use the IWB in front of the class (Q8) and also agreed in their overall preference for IWB-based lessons (Q10). Regarding the responses for the tenth question, a majority of the students reported that they prefer the lessons in which IWBs are used (M=3.21). However, a considerable number of the students (18%) reported having no idea, which may indicate that they felt they did not have enough experience in IWB-based classes to express a sure opinion. Even though slightly more than half of the students expressed the opinion that they like using IWBs in front of the class, a considerable number of the students (25%) also had no idea about this statement, suggesting that they probably had not experienced using the IWBs themselves. In one of the English lessons observed, the students came to the IWB and used it for different purposes such as searching on the Internet, writing, and saving their work, but in many other institutions, both in the observations and in speaking with the teachers, it was learned that only the teachers use this technology. This seems unfortunate, as I learned from the teacher in whose class I observed direct student use of the IWB, that the students liked using it and they did not find it difficult to use. Her report is supported by the students' responses to Question 9, on which two thirds either disagreed or strongly disagreed with the statement that it was difficult for them to use IWBs.

Section 4: Students' Attitudes Related to Motivational Issues

These questions on the questionnaire aimed to investigate students' attitudes related to motivational features deriving from the use of IWBs (see Table 6). The first question in this section explored the students' perceptions related to the idea that IWBs help increase their ability to concentrate on the topic. The second question investigated whether the students feel they participate more in the lessons when an IWB is used. Question 15 intended to learn the students' agreement or disagreement on the notion of whether when an IWB is used students' attention spans are longer. The last question of this section tried to explore the students' attitudes related to the ability of IWBs to make them more motivated.

Table 6: Student's attitudes related to motivational issues

		SD	D	NI	A	SA	Mean*
Q12	f	26	53	94	167	118	3.04
	%	5.68	11.57	20.52	36.46	25.76	
Q13	f	30	65	99	149	115	2.97
	%	6.55	14.19	21.62	32.53	25.11	
Q15	f	27	51	121	158	101	2.94
	%	5.90	11.14	26.42	34.50	22.05	
Q16	f	13	55	98	189	103	2.99
	%	2.84	12.01	21.40	41.27	22.49	

Note: f: Frequency SD: Strongly disagree D: Disagree NI: No idea A: Agree SA: Strongly agree STD: Standard Deviation

Mean*: Means calculated without the NI responses

Q12: I concentrate better when my teacher uses an IWB in English classes.

Q13: I participate in language classes more when my teacher uses an IWB.

Q15: It is easier to keep my attention when an IWB is used during the English classes.

Q16: Use of an IWB makes it easier for me to be motivated during the language classes.

The mean scores calculated showed in Table 6 reveal that the students generally agreed with all the statements in this category. However, the considerable number of students who reported having no idea about these issues indicates that the students have mixed ideas. According to the results of question 12, 62% of the participants believe that they concentrate better when an IWB is used in English classes, either agreeing or strongly agreeing with this statement. For the sixteenth item in this section, again nearly two thirds of the participants agreed that IWB use makes it easier for learners to be motivated during the language classes, and a slight majority of the students agreed that they participate in IWB-based language lessons more than in traditional lessons (58%). In terms of the responses given for the fifteenth item, it is seen that there is truly a mixed divergence of responses. Although 57% of the students agree that IWB use increases their attention span, over a quarter of the students (26%) do not have an idea about this statement. This may indicate that 26% of the students do not feel that IWBs increase their attention span during IWB-based English classes or they have not experienced or felt any increase in terms of attention.

In the open-ended question section, six respondents mentioned the issue of motivation either directly or indirectly. Two respondents stated that the audio and visual materials help them feel more motivated and increase their interest in the lesson. Two students also pointed out that IWBs make lessons more enjoyable and interesting. For instance:

> In my opinion, ... , our lessons are more enjoyable and many of us find IWB-based lessons more interesting (Student 5).

Two participants commented in general that IWBs increase motivation.

Section 5: Students' Attitudes Related to Time Management and Organizational Issues

Three questionnaire items investigated the students' opinions about the features of IWBs in terms of time management and organization of the lessons. The first question in this section aimed to learn the attitudes of the students towards IWBs and a possible resulting increase in the pace of the lesson. Question 18 was related to the organization and plan of the lesson when IWB-based materials are used. The last question of this section investigated the attitudes of the students related to the time saving features of IWBs, which are often noted as one of the basic advantages of IWBs.

Table 7: Students' attitudes related to time management and organizational issues

		SD	D	NI	A	SA	Mean*
Q17	f	113	154	92	60	39	2.05
	%	24.67	33.62	20.09	13.10	8.52	
Q18	f	14	44	95	187	118	3.13
	%	3.06	9.61	20.74	40.83	25.76	
Q19	f	29	39	75	176	139	3.10
	%	6.33	8.52	16.38	38.43	30.35	

Note: f: Frequency SD: Strongly disagree D: Disagree NI: No idea A: Agree SA: Strongly agree STD: Standard Deviation

Mean*: Means calculated without the NI responses

Q17: When my teacher uses an IWB, I cannot keep up with the lesson because the pace of the lesson is much faster.

Q18: The lessons become more organized when an IWB is used.

Q19: Using an IWB saves time.

As is seen in Table 7, the mean scores indicate that the students agreed with the nineteenth and eighteenth items, but they disagreed with question seventeen, which was expressing a negative opinion. When we look at the results of the eighteenth question, 66% of the students believe that when IWBs are used in the lessons, the lessons become more organized, and two thirds of the participants also agreed that IWB use saves time, which is presumably a good thing for teachers and students. However, a considerable number of students responded that they have no idea about these issues. The fairly mixed responses for both of these questions might be because of inefficient use of IWBs by the teachers, leading the students to feel that the lessons are less organized and may or may not save time. The results of the 17th question reveal that 58% of the students feel that they can keep up with the pace of lessons in which IWBs are used.

Section 6: Students' Attitudes Related to the Difference between Traditional Boards and IWBs

In the last section of the first part of the student's questionnaire, two questions were asked, directly related to the differences between traditional boards and IWBs (see Table 8).

Table 8: Students' attitudes related to the difference between traditional boards and IWBs

		SD	D	NI	A	SA	Mean*
Q20	f	85	108	112	99	54	2.32
	%	18.56	23.58	24.45	21.62	11.79	
Q21	f	140	131	61	69	57	2.10
	%	30.57	28.60	13.32	15.07	12.45	

Note: f: Frequency SD: Strongly disagree D: Disagree NI: No idea A: Agree SA: Strongly agree STD: Standard Deviation

Mean*: Means calculated without the NI responses

Q20: There is no difference between my teacher's use of a traditional board and an IWB in terms of teaching techniques and methods.

Q21: I think there is not much difference between an IWB and a normal whiteboard.

The results in Table 8 indicate that the students disagreed with both of the statements in this category, though there are more mixed responses for item 20. The highest number of students selected the "no idea" option for this statement. Of the remainder, the number of the students who disagreed with this statement is higher than the students who agreed that there is no difference between their teacher's use of a traditional board and an IWB in terms of techniques and methods, suggesting in fact a slightly more positive attitude that IWBs are actually different from regular whiteboards. For question 21, 59% of the students thought that there were differences between an IWB and a traditional board. More than half of the students seem to be convinced that IWBs do have functions and extra features over conventional whiteboards.

For responses to the open-ended questions related to this section, two students wrote that there is not much difference between an IWB and a traditional whiteboard and three participants also indicated that IWBs are not helpful. Examples of their comments include:

In my opinion, there is not much difference between an IWB and a traditional whiteboard and I do not think they are useful (Student 35).

All the IWBs should be uninstalled from the school. I can see no difference between an IWB and a traditional whiteboard (Student 13).

Section 7: Factors Affecting Student Attitudes towards IWB Use

In this section, one-way ANOVA tests were performed to explore the relations between the student attitude mean scores and different variables such as age and hours of IWB exposure. These variables were tested against Q10 (I prefer lessons that are taught with an IWB), Q12 (I concentrate better when my teacher uses an IWB), Q1 (I learn more when my teacher uses the IWB), and Q21 (I think there is not much difference between an IWB and a normal whiteboard). The researcher wanted to check whether hours of exposure or age differences could be connected with students' positive attitudes or reported feelings of learning more with IWBs. No significant results were found between age and mean results on the above questions. Only one significant relation was found, between hours of exposure and awareness of the distinctiveness of IWBs (see Table 9).

Table 9: The amount of IWB exposure and feeling the difference between IWBs and traditional whiteboards

		HOURS	Q21
N	Valid	458	458
	Missing	0	0
Mean		2.23	2.5022
Std. Deviation		1.083	1.38332

		Sum of Squares	df	Mean Square	F	Sig.
Q21	Between Groups	41.760	3	13.920	7.589	.000
	Within Groups	832.738	454	1.834		
	Total	874.498	457			

Multiple Comparisons

Dependent Variable: Q21

	(I) HOURS	(J) HOURS	Mean Dif. (I-J)	Std. Error	Sig.	95% Confidence Interval	
						Lower Bound	Upper Bound
Tukey HSD	1-2 hours	3-5 hours	.2222	.13496	.354	-.1260	.5704
		6-10 hours	.4663(*)	.13349	.003	.1219	.8107
		11 and above	.6737(*)	.16098	.000	.2584	1.0890
	3-5 hours	1-2 hours	-.2222	.13496	.354	-.5704	.1260
		6-10 hours	.2441	.14275	.320	-.1242	.6124
		11 and above	.4515(*)	.16874	.039	.0162	.8869

46

6-10 hours	1-2 hours	-.4663(*)	.13349	.003	-.8107	-.1219
	3-5 hours	-.2441	.14275	.320	-.6124	.1242
	11 and above	.2074	.16756	.603	-.2249	.6397
11 and above	1-2 hours	-.6737(*)	.16098	.000	-1.0890	-.2584
	3-5 hours	-.4515(*)	.16874	.039	-.8869	-.0162
	6-10 hours	-.2074	.16756	.603	-.6397	.2249

* The mean difference is significant at the .05 level.

Q21: I think there is not much difference between an IWB and a normal whiteboard.

Table 9 reveals that there is a significant relationship between the amount of IWB exposure and reported belief in the distinctiveness of IWBs over traditional whiteboards. The result may be interpreted that as the hours of IWB-based lessons increase, the degree of recognizing a difference between IWBs and traditional whiteboards rises as well.

Part 2: Teachers' Attitudes towards the Use of Interactive Whiteboards

Section 1: Teachers' Attitudes Related to IWBs as Teaching Tools

The nine questions in this section of the teacher's questionnaire investigated teachers' attitudes towards the use of IWBs as teaching tools. Generally, the proclaimed benefits of IWBs such as saving time, enabling teachers to reach different sources, saving and printing students' work or examples, easing review, and allowing the opportunity to interact with the class face to face were included in the questionnaire statements to learn the teachers' feelings about these features of IWBs. The researcher also wanted to learn whether the teachers feel that they are more effective, efficient, and better managers of their classes when using IWBs.

Table 10: Teacher's attitudes in terms of teaching

		SD	D	NI	A	SA	Mean*
Q1	f	4	7	7	36	28	3.17
	%	4.88	8.54	8.54	43.90	34.15	
Q2	f	8	40	8	18	8	2.35
	%	9.76	48.78	9.76	21.95	9.76	
Q3	f	1	4	8	30	39	3.45
	%	1.22	4.88	9.76	36.59	47.56	
Q4	f	1	7	14	34	26	3.25
	%	1.22	8.54	17.07	41.46	31.71	
Q5	f	1	9	13	35	24	3.19

		SD	D	NI	A	SA	Mean*
	%	1.22	10.98	15.85	42.68	29.27	
Q6	f	2	8	13	37	22	3.14
	%	2.44	9.76	15.85	45.12	26.83	
Q7	f	0	1	7	33	41	3.53
	%	0.00	1.22	8.54	40.24	50.00	
Q8	f	5	9	16	28	24	3.08
	%	6.10	10.98	19.51	34.15	29.27	
Q9	f	0	6	6	32	38	3.42
	%	0.00	7.32	7.32	39.02	46.34	

Note: f: Frequency SD: Strongly disagree D: Disagree NI: No idea A: Agree SA: Strongly agree STD: Standard Deviation

Mean*: Means calculated without the NI responses

Q1: Using the IWB resources reduces the time I spend writing on the board.

Q2: When using IWBs in the classroom, I spend more time for the preparation of the lesson.

Q3: I think using IWBs makes it easier to reach different sources and display them to the whole class immediately.

Q4: IWBs are beneficial for saving and printing the materials generated during the lesson.

Q5: I can give explanations more effectively with the use of IWBs.

Q6: With the help of using the IWB, I can easily control the whole class.

Q7: I think IWBs can be a good supplement to support language teaching.

Q8: Using IWBs makes me a more efficient language teacher.

Q9: Using IWBs makes it easier for a teacher to review, re-explain, and summarize the subject.

According to the mean scores in this table, except for the statement that using IWBs requires more preparation time, the teachers agreed with all statements in this category. The highest mean score belongs to question seven, which indicates that nearly all of the teachers (90%) agree or strongly agree that IWBs can be a good supplement for the language teaching process.

The questions in this section can be categorized into two subcategories: questions related to the benefits of IWBs and questions related directly to the opinions of teachers. Q7 and Q8 can be included in the category of teachers' opinions about IWBs and the rest could be mentioned in the category of benefits and drawbacks of IWBs. Of the second group, the results of the third item show that a majority of the teachers responded positively that IWBs make it easier for them to reach different sources and show them to the whole class at the same time. Regarding the responses related to the ninth question in this section, it can be seen that a majority of the teachers believe that IWBs enable them to review, summarize, and re-explain a subject in an easy way. If we look at the results of the fourth question, we see that 73% of the teachers agreed that IWBs are useful for saving and printing out their students' work. Nearly two thirds of the teachers believe that they can give explanations more effectively by using IWBs. The results of the first question reveal that 78% of the teachers agreed or strongly agreed that using IWB-based resources reduces time spent in writing on the board during the lessons. Looking at the responses given for the sixth question, 72% of the teachers agreed that they could easily control the whole class from the front of the class.

For the second question, which has the lowest mean score in this category, 59% of the teachers disagreed with the idea that preparing for IWB-based lessons takes more time than for a regular lesson. This may indicate that these teachers use special software programs designed for certain textbooks because these programs provide a lot of different activities, exercises, and tests for the teachers, which eases the teachers' job in preparing extra materials. On the other hand, the results also reveal that 32% of the teachers agree with this idea, which suggests that these teachers try to prepare their materials by themselves, so they have to look for special materials and create appropriate materials for IWBs.

In terms of the results of the two questions related to teachers' opinions, nearly two thirds of the teachers agreed with the notion that using IWBs makes them more efficient teachers in the classroom. It is also seen that 90% of the respondents believe that IWBs can be used for supplementing the lessons, resulting in the highest mean score for any question.

Taking the open-ended responses into consideration, three teachers stated that using IWBs saves time for the teacher. Two teachers also reported their feelings that IWB-based lessons are more interesting for the students and therefore the teacher can teach more effectively. In the words of one of these teachers:

> I think this technology is a great opportunity for the students and the teachers because my lessons become more interesting by using IWBs and I can include a great variety of sources (Teacher 7).

On the other hand, one teacher complained that the IWB software that was designed for the course book does not contain anything different from the units of the textbook, so he suggested generally that these supplementary materials should be improved.

Section 2: Teachers' General Attitudes toward the Use of IWBs

These seven questions aimed to investigate teachers' general attitudes towards the use of IWBs. The questions can be divided into subcategories of positive attitudes/feelings and negative attitudes/feelings. Q10 and Q12 may be thought of as positive attitudes because they directly looked at whether the teachers like using this technology and whether they have positive attitudes towards it. On the other hand, Q11, Q13, Q14, and Q16 can be considered as negative attitudes since they explored the negative feelings of the teachers while using IWBs, their negative attitudes towards this technology, their concerns about their students' readiness to use this technology, and doubts about their own readiness to use IWBs. Q15 is directly related to the preference of a traditional way of teaching over IWB technology, so it can be included in the negative category as well.

Table 11: Teacher's attitudes towards the use of IWBs

		SD	D	NI	A	SA	Mean*
Q10	f	2	5	7	31	37	3.37
	%	2.44	6.10	8.54	37.80	45.12	
Q11	f	33	26	9	8	6	1.82
	%	40.24	31.71	10.98	9.76	7.32	
Q12	f	1	5	11	38	27	3.28
	%	1.22	6.10	13.41	46.34	32.93	
Q13	f	37	27	13	4	1	1.55
	%	45.12	32.93	15.85	4.88	1.22	
Q14	f	41	25	6	8	2	1.62
	%	50.00	30.49	7.32	9.76	2.44	
Q15	f	20	31	10	17	4	2.07
	%	24.39	37.80	12.20	20.73	4.88	
Q16	f	45	27	4	4	2	1.53
	%	54.88	32.93	4.88	4.88	2.44	

Note: f: Frequency SD: Strongly disagree D: Disagree N: No idea A: Agree SA: Strongly agree
STD: Standard Deviation
Mean*: Means calculated without the NI responses
Q10: I like using IWB technology in my English classes.
Q11: I feel uncomfortable using IWBs in front of my students.
Q12: I have positive attitudes towards the use of IWBs in language instruction.
Q13: I have negative attitudes towards the use of IWBs in language instruction.
Q14: I do not think my students are ready for this technology.
Q15: What I do in class with traditional methods is sufficient for teaching English.
Q16: I am not the type to do well with IWB-based applications.

In terms of mean scores calculated, the teachers strongly agreed with questions ten and twelve, whereas they disagreed or strongly disagreed with the rest of the questions in this category.

As is seen in Table 11, these remaining questions were actually expressing negative opinions, so the teachers' disagreement with them shows an overall positive attitude, and thus a consistency among the participants' responses is evident.

The results show that the majority of the teachers agreed that they like using IWBs in their lessons, and that they have positive attitudes towards them. Supporting this finding, only 6% of the teachers responded that they have negative attitudes. There is a more mixed response when it comes to the question of whether there is a need for IWBs. Although 61% disagree that their traditional methods are sufficient to teach English, 25% agreed with this statement, which indicates that some teachers do not see the necessity of introducing this new technology into the teaching process. By disagreeing with question 11, the majority of teachers made it clear that using IWBs does not make them uncomfortable in front of their students, and most teachers (72 of the 82 surveyed) were confident that they themselves were suited to using this new technology. Finally, in terms of what the teachers' attitudes towards their students' readiness for IWB use, more than two thirds of the teachers (79%) agreed that their students are 'ready' for this kind of technology.

Section 3: Teachers' Attitudes in terms of Motivational Issues

The questions in this section intended to investigate teachers' attitudes in terms of motivational issues. This section consisted of four questions in total. The questions aimed to gather information about teachers' opinions whether they think that using of IWBs makes lessons more enjoyable and interesting, helps keep the students' attention longer, and increases interaction, motivation, and participation of the students during the lessons.

Table 12: Teacher's attitudes in terms of motivational issues

		SD	D	NI	A	SA	Mean*
Q17	f	1	3	6	32	40	3.46
	%	1.22	3.66	7.32	39.02	48.78	
Q20	f	3	4	11	40	24	3.20
	%	3.66	4.88	13.41	48.78	29.27	
Q21	f	1	7	9	39	26	3.23
	%	1.22	8.54	10.98	47.56	31.71	
Q22	f	1	9	13	32	27	3.23
	%	1.22	10.98	15.85	39.02	32.93	

Note: f: Frequency SD: Strongly disagree D: Disagree N: No idea A: Agree SA: Strongly agree
STD: Standard Deviation
Mean*: Means calculated without the NI responses

Q17: I think IWBs make language learning more enjoyable and more interesting.

Q20: I can keep my students' attention longer with the help of IWB technology in language classes.

Q21: I think IWBs increase the interaction and participation of the students in English classes.

Q22: I think my students are more motivated when I use an IWB in my English classes.

The mean scores and low standard deviations calculated show that the teachers agreed or strongly agreed with all the statements in this category. The mean score of question seventeen is the highest (M=3.46), which indicates that nearly all of the teachers (almost 88%) agreed that IWBs make lessons more enjoyable and interesting. Nearly 80% of the participating teachers agreed that the use of IWBs increases the interaction and participation of the students, and nearly two thirds of the teachers believe that their students are more motivated when an IWB is used in the classroom. The responses given for the 22nd question in this category show that 78% of the EFL teachers agreed that they can keep their students' attention longer when they use IWBs during the lessons.

Two of the participants wrote in positive extra comments, stating that IWBs attract the students' attention and increase student participation. On the other hand, two other teachers observed that when the classroom lights are dimmed, some of the students lose attention:

> When the classroom is a bit dark, my students start to sleep and lose their
> concentration. I think only the curtains near the IWB should be closed and the back of
> the classroom might get light from outside so that students do not tend to sleep
> (Teacher 19).

In order to avoid loss of attention when the lights are dimmed, the curtains at the back of the classroom can be opened or the lights could be switched on at the back of the classroom so that darkness of the classroom does not affect the students negatively.

Section 4: Teachers' Attitudes Related to the Issue of Training

The last category of the teacher's questionnaire contained two questions addressing the specific issue of training for the use of IWBs: whether it is necessary and whether without it, they still feel comfortable using IWBs (see Table 12).

Table 13: Teacher's attitudes related to the training issue

		SD	D	NI	A	SA	Mean*
Q18	f	1	12	17	34	18	3.06
	%	1.22	14.63	20.73	41.46	21.95	
Q19	f	5	23	12	30	12	2.70
	%	6.10	28.05	14.63	36.59	14.63	

Note: f: Frequency SD: Strongly disagree D: Disagree N: No idea A: Agree SA: Strongly agree

STD: Standard Deviation

Mean*: Means calculated without the NI responses

Q18: I believe that training is required to teach with IWB technology.

Q19: If I do not get sufficient training, I do not feel comfortable with using IWBs in the classroom.

The mean scores reveal that the teachers believe in the need for training, but are much more divided over whether such training is absolutely necessary in order for them to feel comfortable using IWBs. According to the responses given for the 18th question, 63% of the participants agreed that training is necessary for the use of this technology. For question 19 however, there is a more mixed response. Although 34% of the EFL teachers report that they feel comfortable without any training while using an IWB, 51% of the respondents agreed that they do feel uncomfortable, if they do not get sufficient training. Since the agreement score is higher than the disagreement rate, it can be said that the need for training is accepted as an important issue.

One of the teachers made the point that teachers themselves have a role to play in getting ready to use IWBs:

> I agreed with the training requirement, but this is a skill that teachers must develop
> themselves, make time to explore this technology and its potential. If they do not
> make time, they will not use it effectively (Teacher 16).

This opinion indicates that it is the teachers' responsibility in part to learn to use this technology, but the administrators should also encourage teachers and plan training sessions for them. The comment may suggest that if a teacher does not have positive attitudes towards this technology or believe in its benefits, it might be difficult for him/her to become accustomed to using it.

Section 5: Factors Affecting Teacher Attitudes towards IWB Use

In this section, one-way ANOVA tests were performed to explore the relation between teacher attitudes and different variables such as age, experience, and hours of IWB use. The researcher wanted to check whether hours of IWB use, age differences, and experience of teachers can be connected to positive attitudes or negative attitudes. Correlations were sought between hours of IWB use, age, and experience variables and questions 10 (I like using IWB technology in my lessons), Q12 (I have positive attitudes towards the use of IWBs in language instruction), Q13 (I have negative attitudes towards the use of IWBs in language instruction), and Q15 (What I do in class with traditional methods is sufficient in teaching English). After ANOVA tests were performed, none of the relations were found to be significant except for that between hours of IWB use and liking the use of IWB technology.

Table 14: ANOVA results for hours of teachers' IWB use and positive attitude towards IWBs

		HOURS	Q10
N	Valid	82	82
	Missing	0	0
Mean		2,7561	3,3733
Std. Deviation		1,29158	,73104

		Sum of Squares	df	Mean Square	F	Sig.
Q10	Between Groups	19.183	3	6.394	8.254	.000
	Within Groups	60.427	78	.775		
	Total	79.610	81			

Note: The number of hours of using IWBs.

Q10: I like using IWB technology in my lessons

Multiple Comparisons

Dependent Variable: Q10

	(I) HOURS	(J) HOURS	Mean Difference (I-J)	Std. Error	Sig.	95% Confidence Interval	
						Lower Bound	Upper Bound
Tukey HSD	1-2 hours	3-5 hours	-.5833	.25150	.103	-1.2450	.0784
		6-10 hours	-.6667	.28676	.102	-1.4211	.0878

54

		11 and above	-.7613(*)	.19393	.001	-1.2715	-.2510
3-5 hours	1-2 hours		.5833	.25150	.103	-.0784	1.2450
	6-10 hours		-.0833	.30803	.993	-.8937	.7271
	11 and above		-.1779	.22419	.857	-.7678	.4119
6-10 hours	1-2 hours		.6667	.28676	.102	-.0878	1.4211
	3-5 hours		.0833	.30803	.993	-.7271	.8937
	11 and above		-.0946	.26313	.984	-.7869	.5977
11 and above	1-2 hours		.7613(*)	.19393	.001	.2510	1.2715
	3-5 hours		.1779	.22419	.857	-.4119	.7678
	6-10 hours		.0946	.26313	.984	-.5977	.7869

* The mean difference is significant at the .05 level.

The result in Table 13 shows that there is a significant relationship between the hours of the teachers' IWB use and the degree of liking the use of IWBs. Specifically, post hoc tests reveal a significant difference between the group with the lowest exposure (1-2 hours) and the group with the highest exposure (11+ hours). In general, what this suggests is that as the number of hours of using IWBs increases, teachers' rating of how much they like using this technology increases as well. This is an important finding because as the teachers explore this technology day by day, its potential and difference from traditional whiteboards are seen by the teachers and they want to use it more often. It is also related to the feedback coming from the students because when the teachers hear positive feedback, they want to use this technology more enthusiastically, as one of the administrators noted in the interview.

Part 3: Interviews with the Administrators

Interviews were carried out with administrators of three universities, in which there are English teaching preparatory programs. Two of the institutions were private and the third was a state university. There were six questions asked of the interviewees. The aim of the interview was to explore the attitudes of administrators towards the use of IWBs in their institutions and to see whether they were supportive or critical of this technology.

The first question was designed to investigate whether the administrators thought that technology use in general is necessary for EFL teachers or not. When analyzing the responses given for this question, it is seen that all of the interviewees agreed that technology use is absolutely necessary for EFL teachers for the general reason that teachers must not fall behind technological advances in this era of information and computer technologies. However, one of the interviewees added the cautionary point that technology should carry a clear educational purpose and it should be used in a purposeful way.

> Of course, it is necessary, but it should serve a purpose. For example, technology should not used for only entertainment and it should be used with an intention related to teaching (Interviewee 2).

In other words, technology can be a helpful aid, but teachers should be selective when incorporating technological facilities in their lessons, and take care to insure that those technological aids are used appropriately in order to enhance teaching.

The second question aimed to explore the administrators' observations about the extent of technology use by EFL teachers at their institutions. Two of the interviewees responded that since their institutions are private, it is obligatory for them to provide and use enough technological investments in order to impress their students. However, even though their technological infrastructure is high, the administrators complained that the teachers working at those institutions have not benefited from technology as much as was expected. One of the interviewee talked about the ups and downs teachers had experienced when the new technology was introduced:

> It was not easy at first, of course. However, when they have become accustomed to the new technology, got nice and positive feedback from the students, and seen the lessons are more interesting and lively, they like this technology now. It was in a way mutual. Even though the teachers were hesitant at first, the role of decreasing the teachers' burden helped them like the technology (Interviewee 2).

From this expression, we can understand that the administrators' encouragement, positive reactions of the different stakeholders, and hands-on experiencing of the potential of IWB technology can help encourage teachers' positive feelings towards IWBs or any new technological tool.

The third question was intended to learn in what concrete ways the administrators support the use of IWBs. Two of the interviewees stated that they support the use of this technology by providing technical support, financial support, and verbal encouragement. They also pointed out that they get financial support and recommendations coming from the higher administrators in their institutions. Two of the respondents indicated that they get some support from the publishers in the form of providing IWB software for certain course books, training, and extra materials, which makes the teachers' job easier. One of the administrators stated that she had a teacher who is familiar with this technology and that teacher voluntarily provided training for her colleagues:

> One of our teachers, as far as I know, has taken a special training. And she planned a training program for her colleagues. Each of our teachers, either one by one or in

56

groups of two, got training from her. She also helped the teachers when they had problems with the system and the IWBs (Interviewee 2).

One of the interviewees declared that they were planning a special in-service training session in order to train all the teachers. The interviewee from the state university stated that they chose one of the colleagues to be responsible for the smart class and she also provides a kind of support for other teachers.

The next question aimed to elicit the factors affecting the administrators' decision to purchase this technology. One of the respondents stated that this technology was first installed in the physics department and then was proposed by the rector to be installed in the school of foreign languages, so the decision was not initiated by the foreign languages school itself. Another participant pointed out that the support given by the publisher was very important for the institution and it encouraged the administration to purchase this technology. If the software had not been prepared and presented to them, they would not have installed this technology. The third participant's response was similar to the second, though she added that the teachers' reactions and opinions also played an important role in persuading the administration to install this technology.

The fifth question was asked in order to learn the most common problems that the EFL teachers reported facing while using this technology. All of the interviewees declared that technical problems are the most frequent problems they are told about. One of the problems is that the batteries run out of energy in a short time. According to one respondent, another problem is the complaint about the use of the special pen that fails to write on the IWB or is difficult to write with. Another participant pointed out that there is frequently a need for recalibrating the device, which wastes time and causes a loss of students' motivation if this problem occurs in the middle of the lesson. The last problem that they complained about was having the screen freeze, in which case nothing can be done. If this problem occurs, the teacher has to turn off the system and re-start it.

For the last question, the respondents were asked to talk about the benefits of IWB technology for language teaching purposes in particular. All of the participants expressed their beliefs that IWB-based lessons are more interesting, enjoyable, and different from traditional lessons due in part to the use of audio and visual materials, which attract the students' attention and increase their motivation. The interviewee from the state university declared that thanks to the use of IWBs, students' images about his institution as a whole had become more positive and they had started to think that their school is "the best". Another respondent stated that this technology increases the amount of interaction between the teacher and the students, is good for class management, and appeals to different learning styles:

57

It is absolutely helpful. First, I believe that there is more interaction with IWBs because you do not have to turn your back to the students. While using IWBs, you are always facing your students, which increases the amount of contact with the students. Second, it is advantageous for time management because you do not have to use chalk and duster anymore and your materials are ready in the software. Third, this technology works with different intelligence type students such as visual, kinesthetic, and aural (Interviewee 3).

She also added that since duster and chalk are not used any more, IWBs increase the cleanliness of the classrooms. One important thing that she stated was that using this technology makes it possible to include all types of intelligences during the lessons. All the students are involved in the lessons and different types of activities and materials may make it possible to help all of them understand topics more easily.

Part 4: EFL Teachers' Actual Use of IWB Technology

According to the literature on IWBs, IWBs have many benefits such as increasing teaching time by using ready materials (Walker, 2003), increasing motivation and interaction (Gerard et al., 1999; Levy, 2002), reducing the need for note taking (BECTA, 2003), permitting the saving and printing out of students' work (Walker, 2002), and so on. In order to see whether the teachers take benefit from these claimed features and whether they encounter any problems related to this technology, the researcher conducted observations of three different lessons in which IWBs are used. These observations were also intended to reveal the different uses of this technology between institutions, and allow for first-hand observations of the reactions of the students and teachers towards this technology. The type of IWB that was used in the high school observed was the active whiteboard (electromagnetic). This board was the most functional one compared to others observed. However, the one used in the university was passive whiteboard that had basic functions and it was not connected to the Internet. This difference limits the actual uses of IWBs by the teachers. In this section, three lessons are described in detail to show the ways that teachers and students use IWB technology.

The first English class observed was in a state university. The lesson was mainly focused on reading, but also had parts related to writing skills. The teacher handed out worksheets including a task in which the students were asked to choose correct topic sentences and complete missing parts of paragraphs. First, students were given four or five minutes to choose appropriate choices from multiple-choice items. They circled the best answer on their worksheets and waited for the teacher. The teacher showed the same word document on the IWB, and asked the students which choice was the correct answer. After hearing the answers, she circled the correct answer by clicking on a pencil icon marked in yellow. She was then able to highlight the answer in yellow by using her finger. Next, she circled the wrong answers coming from the students in red. After that she went on to highlight main ideas and supporting ideas with different colors so that students could identify important points, which helped them to more easily find the topic sentence among the choices. At the end of this procedure, the students who chose wrong answers were able to see where they had made mistakes because everything was clear on the IWB screen in different colors. The lesson went on in the same format until the end. This observation revealed that the teacher used the IWB mainly for showing materials and highlighting the important points on the IWB screen. This can be evaluated as one of the basic uses of an IWB.

A second lesson was observed in a high school English reading class. The class was made up of intermediate level students who were following a course book throughout the semester. At the start of the lesson, one of the students was asked to turn on the system, open Internet Explorer, and go to the Google web page. There was a special keyboard on the screen and the student used it for writing the letters and numbers. On this web site, the student wrote the name of the author of the passage they were reading, and found his biography. The class scanned some important information about him, such as a reward he had won and other details about his life. The teacher then opened a blank page. The teacher asked the students to answer some reading comprehension questions and had them write the answers on the IWB one by one. Various students came to the board and wrote the answers using the special pen. When the page was full, the lead student ticked an arrow and a new blank page appeared. Using the save function, all the written pages were able to be saved, and the class was able to go back to those pages again. For the next part of the lesson, the teacher wrote some examples about Past Continuous Tense and Simple Past Tense on the IWB in order to revise these tenses. The class then started to work on a grammar exercise in the book and the students gave the answers for the blanks. While doing this activity, one of the students asked the meaning of the word "jaws". The teacher immediately asked another student to come up to find the "seslisözlük" web site for the dictionary. The student opened the page and wrote the word in the address bar. When the meaning appeared on the page, the teacher pressed the sign for pronunciation of that word and the class heard its pronunciation. The students not only saw the Turkish meaning, but also its meaning in English. After all the answers for the grammar exercise were written on the IWB, the teacher went on with phrasal verb practice. The lesson ended with the teacher's giving homework. In this lesson, many examples of the functional use of IWBs can be seen, such as using extra sources via the Internet, playing audio materials, writing and saving, and using an online dictionary.

The third lesson observed was a writing class for upper-intermediate university students. The topic of the lesson was organizational patterns of an argumentative paragraph. The teacher started the lesson by explaining the difference between an "opponent" and a "proponent". She showed a sample paragraph on the IWB screen and asked the students to say which part reflects "opponent" and which part belongs to "proponent". Then she highlighted the transitional signals in the paragraph and used square brackets to separate the parts of the paragraph with green. After that, she drew an outline of this paragraph on the traditional board. While highlighting and writing, she used her finger by pressing on one of the icons on the right side of the screen. She did not use a special pen for writing on the IWB. Next, she showed the second paragraph that was in a different format and followed the same procedure to present it. By clicking on the screen, she changed the page and presented another text. The lesson continued in this manner and ended with an overall summary of all organizational types, in which there were arrows showing the similarities and differences of each paragraph format.

All the observation data gathered to see the actual use of IWBs in English language classes showed that effective use of IWBs depends on the features of the IWBs and the particular system installed. For instance, when a teacher wants to search for extra information, there should be Internet access made available with the IWB, otherwise, this function does not work and the students cannot benefit from this opportunity. Some IWB trademarks allow other functions that were not observed in this study, for instance, voting. With this function for example, the teacher shows a test on the IWB, the students can send their votes for the correct answer by using small hand-held tools. After all the votes are collected, the system shows the results on the screen and the teacher can then explain the correct answer. Highlighting is clearly another main function that is well suited to use with IWBs. The teacher can easily use different colors to underline important points in a written text. Moreover, the teacher or the students do not have to erase the written items on the IWB because when you click on "next page" it provides a new blank page. It is also possible to then save and print all of your examples and as well as the students' work. This appears to be a possibility that is unique to this technology. In one of the classes observed, the students came up to the IWB and used it themselves for writing answers and searching for the meanings of words on the Internet. With a traditional whiteboard, this latter function is not possible and the teachers have to write the meaning of an unknown word on the board by himself/herself, which may be time consuming and also may lead to a more teacher-centered lesson.

Along with the benefits and advantages of IWBs, there are also some problems and drawbacks of this technology. I noticed in one of the lessons that sunlight did make it hard to see the texts and images on the screen of the IWB. Many students stated this problem in the open-ended section of student's questionnaire and their complaints seem warranted. Another important issue about IWB technology is the distribution of IWBs and traditional whiteboards. In one of the institutions observed, all the classrooms had IWBs installed and there were no normal whiteboards for alternative use. In the second institution, there was only one classroom installed with an IWB. If the classrooms are not all equipped with IWBs, some of the students complain about having to change classrooms.

Lastly, it is worth noting that during the three classes observed, I did not witness any technical problems. This may be coincidental, but it seems that technical problems are not encountered very often while using IWBs. I asked the classroom teachers about the technical problems faced and one stated that they had not yet faced any problem during this year. However, administrators pointed out that sometimes teachers come to them and ask for technical help when the IWB freezes or the pen does not work.

Conclusion

This chapter presented the data analysis of the students', teachers', and administrators' attitudes towards the use of IWB technology in EFL context. Qualitative data gathered by interviews with the administrators and observations of IWB-based English lessons were also presented. In the next chapter, the findings will be discussed in detail and in parallel with the findings in the literature.

CHAPTER V: CONCLUSION

Overview of the Study

This study investigated the attitudes of students, EFL teachers, and administrators towards the use of IWBs, factors affecting students' and teachers' attitudes positively or negatively, and the actual use of IWBs in language classes. Both qualitative and quantitative data were collected during this study. The participants of the study were selected from a variety of students who have experienced IWB technology in English classes, teachers who have used this technology in their lessons, and three administrators from different educational institutions in which IWB technology is used. In order to elicit the students' and the teachers' attitudes towards the use of IWBs, two different questionnaires were used. Four hundred fifty-eight students and eighty-two EFL teachers responded to the questionnaires in this study. Interviews were also conducted with administrators to explore their attitudes towards the use of IWBs. One-hour English lessons at three different institutions were observed to gain initial insights into the ways of IWB use in language instruction settings. The research questions addressed in this analysis were as follows:

1) What are the attitudes of Turkish EFL teachers towards interactive whiteboards?
2) What are the attitudes of Turkish EFL students towards interactive whiteboards?

3) What are the attitudes of administrators in Turkish educational contexts towards interactive whiteboards?

4) How are IWBs used in EFL classrooms in Turkey?

5) What factors may influence Turkish students' and teachers' attitudes towards the use of IWBs in EFL classrooms?

This chapter will present and discuss the findings and implications drawn from the results of data analysis in relationship to the existing literature on IWB use and their incorporation into English classes. The findings will be presented and discussed under four headings:

1- Students' and teachers' attitudes and feelings towards the use of IWBs in English classes.

2- Administrators' attitudes towards the use of IWBs.

3- Factors affecting students' and teachers' attitudes towards the use of IWBs in English instruction.

4- Actual use of IWBs in English classes.

After the presentation and discussion of the findings, pedagogical implications and limitations of the study will be clarified, and in light of the conclusions from this study, suggestions for further research will be made.

Discussion of the Results

Attitudes of Students and Teachers towards the Use of IWBs in Language Learning Settings

The items in the second part of the student and teacher questionnaires were designed to investigate the attitudes of both groups towards the use of IWBs in English lessons. The questionnaire items were categorized according to particular concepts in order to ease reporting and analysis. The six categories were: learning and teaching; affective factors and attitudes; motivational issues; technical issues; differences between IWBs and traditional whiteboards; and training.

Section 1: Student and Teacher Attitudes Related to Learning and Teaching

In this section, the results indicate that both students and teachers think that IWBs are useful devices for enhancing teaching and learning processes and both groups expressed their positive opinions about the contribution of this technology, and its use of audio and visual materials in particular, to language teaching. These generally positive reports are in line with the results of previous attitude studies about IWBs. In Wall et al.'s (2005) study, the majority of the pupils surveyed also expressed their positive opinions about the IWBs' contribution to effective learning.

In the same study, more than half of the pupils mentioned how the IWB assisted their understanding with the help of visuals, different software programs, and games. Most of the student comments in Glover and Miller's (2001) study also supported this idea that IWB-based lessons are easier to follow and may help the students who have difficulty in understanding the lessons. The responses in the current study that gained the highest mean scores were question 4 (Using audio and visual materials with IWBs helps me understand the lesson better.) and question 14 (IWBs make learning more interesting and exciting.), which reveals that both having the opportunity of using audio and visual materials and creating interesting and exciting lessons are two characteristics of IWBs which are appreciated by the students. The results in this study revealed that a majority of the students agreed that when audio and visual materials are used with IWBs, they can understand lessons better and feel that they learn more.

Regarding the teachers' responses related to teaching, the teachers strongly agreed that IWBs are a good supplement for teaching and that IWBs make it easier to show different kinds of materials to the class. In Levy (2002) and Lee and Boyle (2004), the teachers reported that IWBs make it easier to draw on a greater number and wider variety of information and learning sources and these sources can be used flexibly and spontaneously in response to different pedagogical needs. The findings in the current study agree with this notion that it is esier to reach different sources with IWBs and that the whole class can benefit from these sources at the same time. Teachers in the current study also strongly agreed with the idea that the use of IWBs makes it possible to review, re-explain, and summarize a topic easily and effectively, since the saved or ready examples from the previous lessons and a great variety of other sources make it easier for the teacher to re-present the subject. This is similar to points raised in earlier studies. Most of the students in Glover and Miller's (2001) study, for example, reported that with the help of IWBs, their teachers were able to review things if they needed to study them again. More than two thirds of the teachers in that study also agreed with the idea that the opportunity to save and print out the students' work and other materials is a very useful facility of IWBs, and is in fact a feature unique to IWBs, a point noted in both Walker (2002) and Lee and Boyle (2004).

The only statement in this category that the teachers disagreed with was one suggesting that preparation of IWB-based lessons takes more time than for a regular lesson. This finding contradicts with a participant's comment in Glover and Miller's (2001) study that IWBs require earlier and better preparation from teachers. Levy's (2002) study also revealed that most of the teachers felt that initial lesson planning and materials preparation such as nice flipcharts take a long time to prepare. According to the findings in Moss et al. (2007), teachers reported preparing their own resources 78% of the time, and 42% of the time using commercial software. Although the findings in that study indicate that the teachers mostly spend a long time to prepare their own materials, this study may indicate that Turkish EFL teachers are either using commercial software or are finding prepared IWB materials on the Internet since they report that it is not time consuming to prepare IWB-based materials. Although in the observations I conducted, there were not any teachers who used a software program, but the researcher knows that some teachers use software programs specially designed for certain course books, such as Face2Face. Since the number of observations is limited to three, it was not possible to verify the use of software programs in English classes.

Section 2: Student's Attitudes Related to Affective Factors and Teachers' General Attitudes towards IWBs

In this section, students' opinions related to affective factors and teachers' attitudes towards the use of IWB were analyzed together since these statements in the questionnaires reflected their overall preferences, concerns, and positive or negative attitudes. Since the attitudes of students and teachers are important to understand the potential of IWB technology, the results in this section are significant in that they reveal that students and teachers are positive about this technology. For instance, the majority of the students prefer IWB-based lessons and more than two thirds of the teachers like using IWBs. Both the results of Levy (2002) and Smith (1999) are similar to this finding in that the learners in these studies appreciated visual presentations, and the interesting atmosphere of an IWB-based lesson. However, comparing the percentages of responses to these ideas, it is seen that the degree of the teachers' liking to use IWBs is higher than the degree of the students' preference for this technology. Here one may question something also mentioned in Wall et al.'s (2005) and Smith et al.'s (2005) articles – which is the question of who is actually using the IWB. Although students are eager to come up and write on the board, not all teachers allow their students to interact with the IWB. This may cause students to feel that they cannot feel the real distinctiveness of IWB technology and may lower their interest. From the teachers' perspective, it can be said that once teachers have experienced the unique features or benefits of IWBs, they like them more and try to incorporate them into their teaching contexts.

Additionally, in informal conversation with some of the teachers, it emerged that their students are sometimes more enthusiastic and ready for using this technology than the teachers themselves and sometimes some students help their teachers while using this technology. This indicates that this technology has already been accepted and appreciated by the students even though there could be a few students in each institution who might reject the use of this technology.

In general, a majority of the teachers also reported having positive attitudes towards IWBs, and like using this technology. This finding is again in line with Levy's (2002) study, in which the teachers reported positive attitudes, highlighting specifically the educational benefits of IWBs and the role they can play in motivating students, increasing participation, and focusing students' attention. Another result of this study revealed that the majority of the teachers expressed their readiness to use this technology, which speaks optimistically for the eventual spreading of this technology among other language teaching institutions. When we look for studies about readiness to use IWBs, the results seem restricted to the readiness of students. Seven of the pupil groups in Hall and Higgins (2005) commented that it takes only a week or so to get used to IWBs. That comment shows that students are ready to use IWB technology in their lessons since they are experiencing technological advances and facilities maybe more than teachers do, so the adaptation of students to IWB technology may not be so difficult. One of the teachers also told me that some of her students are better than she is at using IWBs and sometimes the students solve technical problems by themselves.

Section 3: Students' and Teachers' Attitudes Related to Motivational Issues

When we come to the results related to motivational issues, a large number of students agreed that IWBs help them feel motivated, increase their concentration, and make them feel that they participate more in lessons. This finding supports the finding in Wall et al. (2005) in which 80% of the primary school students commented that IWBs have a positive impact on motivation. As some of the students wrote in their comments in the open-ended section of the student questionnaire in this study, IWB use with audio and visual materials increases students' motivation and helps them keep their attention longer. In Wall et al (2005), most of the students also made positive statements about the role of IWBs' motivational contributions and in making the lessons more interesting and fun. The results of Weimer (2001) revealed that the degree of the students' motivation increased with the use of IWBs, which would be parallel with the reported opinions of the students in this study. All findings indicate that IWBs are perceived as good motivators in teaching and learning contexts by the students and this motivational power can affect students' achievement positively and reinforce learning.

As for the teachers, nearly all agreed that they felt IWBs make their lessons more interesting and enjoyable for the students. This finding supports the results of Levy (2002), in which all the teachers felt that students enjoy IWB-based lessons more than regular lessons and tend to be more interested in the IWB-based lessons. In Hall and Higgins (2005), it was stated that students enjoy the lessons in which IWBs are used because of the multi-media capabilities and the opportunity to play games with IWBs. With regard to other motivational issues in this study, nearly two thirds of the teachers agreed that IWBs increase the motivation, interaction, and participation of the students. This finding is also in parallel with the comments made by the secondary school teachers in Levy

65

(2002), in which some teachers stated that IWBs have a positive impact on the students' motivation to learn. One of the English teachers in Glover and Miller (2001) commented that IWBs motivate the students differently from books in terms of the way IWBs engage the students and attract their attention. The results both in this study and earlier studies indicate that a majority of the teachers report that IWBs help the learners be motivated and be attentive to the lessons. These are significant factors in the teaching process because when students are motivated and attentive to the lesson, it is easier and more effective to teach new topics and arguably even improves students' retention of the material taught.

Section 4: Students' Attitudes Related to Technical Issues

In terms of technical issues, not being able to see the things displayed on the IWB screen because of sunlight is a common problem not only stated through the responses given to Q6, but also through open-ended responses. This issue is also raised in Hall and Higgins's (2005) study. There, several of the pupil groups also complained about the sunlight issue, adding that the window blinds were not big enough to block out the light totally.

The results of question seven (IWBs often break down and recalibration causes a waste of time) show that although a slightly larger group of students disagreed with the idea that IWBs frequently break down and thereby cause a waste of time, a quarter of the participants had no idea about this problem and 32% of the students agreed with this idea. This may indicate that the plurality of the students has not faced IWB breakdowns or if they have, that these problems were solved in a short time. This finding contradicts with Levy's (2002) study in which many students drew attention to technical failures that disrupt IWB-based lessons. Both in Levy's (2002) and Glover and Miller's (2001) studies, some other technical problems such as lack of response of the electronic pen, inability to manipulate certain images and symbols, and freezing of the screen are mentioned prominently. Possibly, improvements in the hardware have moderated these problems somewhat. When these problems do occur, however, IWBs need recalibration, switching off and on, or some external help to overcome these technical problems. It is advisable therefore, for teachers to be ready for these problems with extra materials so that if they occur, the teaching and learning process is not affected.

Section 5: Students' Attitudes Related to the Differences between Traditional Boards and IWBs

Two questionnaire items raised doubts about the distinctiveness of IWBs from traditional white boards. By disagreeing with both of the statements in this category, the students acknowledged that there are differences between traditional boards and IWBs. The results also revealed that the students recognized the difference between their teachers' teaching techniques when they are using IWB technology and when they use traditional teaching methods. This finding is important because some of the teachers and administrators may think that LCD projectors and IWBs are similar, so there is no need to install IWBs in the classrooms. According to some teachers, traditional white boards may seem adequate for teaching. The researcher also thinks that if IWB technology had been more widespread and used for a longer time at schools, the students and teachers might have been even stronger in their reporting of the benefits of IWBs and in noticing the benefits afforded by IWB-based lessons. The result of an ANOVA test in the previous chapter supports this idea since it showed that as the hours of IWB-based lessons increase, the degree of recognizing differences between IWBs and regular whiteboards rises as well.

Section 6: Attitudes of Teachers towards the Training Issues

One of the frequent issues raised by many teachers is the need for adequate training in order to benefit from all of the IWBs' potential. According to the results of this study, 63% of the teachers agreed that they need training to use this technology. This finding is not surprising since it is similar to that in Glover and Miller (2001). In their study, one third of the teachers found it difficult to figure out the techniques of IWB use and to plan the lessons. If we refer to one student's statement in Levy's (2002) study, we get an interesting insight into how teachers should use this technology appropriately and effectively:

I prefer normal boards because the teachers do not act clever using IWBs.

In other words, teachers should be confident and "clever" in using IWB functions and they should not use IWBs just for presentations or similar to the ways of using traditional boards.

Although 36% of the teachers in this study report that they feel comfortable in using an IWB without any training, 48% of the respondents said that lack of training makes them feel uncomfortable. All in all, these results indicate that a fairly large group of the participating teachers seems to have found IWBs not difficult to use, and feel that without special training they can still use it and in a sense train themselves, but training is still an important service to be offered. Dexter, Anderson, and Becker's (1999) study revealed that provision of efficient and effective training support is important for the systematic incorporation of any new technology into education settings. In Levy (2002), it was stated that the teachers with less confidence about IT may not be able to train themselves and they may need more sustained and individual support in terms of training before using IWB technology. One of the respondents in that study pointed out that it is not "training" when someone simply gives someone else a booklet about the technology. It is advisable that teachers who want to use this technology, regardless of whether or not they feel that they have enough knowledge about computers, should be given the opportunity to take focused training to learn how to exploit all of the functions of IWBs during the teaching process.

When it comes to administrators' opinions about technology and IWB use in language instruction settings, they think that EFL teachers absolutely need to benefit from technological advances. It is critical to ensure however that the "new" things are truly useful and important for improved language instruction and learning, and are not just new fads, or just slightly new ways of doing the same old things. As mentioned in Higgins, Beauchamp, and Miller's (2007) literature review on IWBs, even though the use of IWBs might change the way that learning takes place, IWBs may not have a significant impact on achievement. This shows that effective and successful teaching continues to depend on teachers' abilities, creativity, and intent in general. For instance, a "bad" teacher using the special functions on an IWB is not going to be as effective as a "good" teacher without extra materials to work with. Therefore, technology should be used cleverly, but without letting the flashy new tool overshadow what is being done with it.

One of the interview questions investigated whether the administrators support the use of this technology in their institutions. All of the respondents interpreted this question as referring largely to technical support and indicated that they provide technical support in the form of technicians for when problems arise, spending money for increasing the quality of the technological infrastructure of the classrooms, and assigning some specially trained teachers to train their colleagues and thereby increase the number of teachers who use this technology. One of the interviewees also stated that they are planning training sessions for all of the teachers in her institution. These statements show that all of the administrators support their personnel's use of IWB technology.

In terms of the factors affecting the administrators' decisions to purchase this technology, two of the interviewees reported that both the students' and teachers' positive feedback and publishers' support played a role in their decision making process. Since IWB-based software programs prepared by publishers and designed for course books provide relevant and ready materials, teachers are often eager to benefit from these programs and this willingness may affect administrators' decisions to buy this technology. Teachers' positive feedback about the actual use of new technology may also influence administrators' decisions. As one of the respondents stated that this technology investment was made on the advice and with the financial support of the university rector, it is sometimes possible to see that decisions about investment in IWB technology may be made by other administrators. If decisions come from above, there could be a risk of rejection of new things by the users and the decisions may not be consistent with the actual needs of the teachers and the learners. Additionally, provision of new advances may not yield expected results if there is insufficient training support for the staff on how to incorporate the new technology into their teaching contexts.

Another finding related to administrators' attitudes towards the use of IWBs is their reported shared belief that IWBs are useful and effective tools for education. All of the administrative respondents were convinced that IWBs make lessons more enjoyable and interesting for the students. A variety of materials and resources help more students become involved in the lessons, and make it possible to address different intelligences at the same time. When we turn to the teachers' use of IWB, one of the administrators talked about the importance of interaction between the teachers and the students and added that classroom management is easier with IWBs since the teacher does not have to turn his/her back to the class.

All of these statements indicate that the administrators are supportive of the use of IWB technology and they try to help their personnel to learn and benefit from this technology. Here it should also be taken into consideration that while there is not so much financial concern among the institutions that are owned by companies or investors, state schools and universities depend on limited budgets. Even if the administrators want to install this technology in every classroom, it is not necessarily possible without outside financial income, funds, or sponsors.

Factors Affecting Teacher and Student Attitudes towards IWB Use

In this section of the study, one-way ANOVA tests were performed to explore the relations between respondent attitudes and different variables such as age, experience, and hours of IWB use. In terms of the teachers, it was speculated that hours of IWB use, age differences, and work experience may affect their attitudes towards the use of IWBs. These factors were therefore correlated with questions about liking IWB technology, having certain attitudes towards the use of IWBs, and finding traditional methods sufficient for teaching English. Statistically, only the relationship between hours of actual IWB use and liking the use of IWB technology was found to be significant. This finding indicates that as the number of hours of using IWBs increases, teachers' rating of how much they like using this technology increases as well. This finding reveals that as the teachers experience the unique features of IWBs, they like this technology more and feel more positive about it. The literature on IWBs has not yet given us a similar result to this, so this is a new and previously unnoted finding in the literature and it is one that IWB manufacturers will no doubt be happy to hear about.

With regard to the factors affecting the students' attitudes, correlations were sought between their attitudes and different variables such as age, type of school, and hours of IWB exposure. Again only one significant relation was found, this time between hours of exposure and awareness of the distinctiveness of IWBs. The result showed that as the hours of student exposure to IWB-based lessons increases, the degree of recognizing a difference between IWBs and traditional whiteboards rises as well. This finding is not mentioned in the existing IWB literature and is significant to the extent that it shows students' growing awareness of the distinctiveness of this technology and its potential.

The results of question 8 (I like going to the front of the class to use an IWB) in the student questionnaire might be included in this section since its results may be related to age. The finding revealed that though slightly more than half of the participants agreed that they like using IWBs in front of the class, 10% of the students declared that they did not like using IWBs in front of the class. It seems possible that these mixed comments might be related to age. Young learners may like using this technology by touching on the screen and writing with the special pen as some of the primary schools students' commented in Hall and Higgins (2005). However, adult learners may find it more unusual and therefore difficult to use this technology and may fear losing face in front of their peers if they cannot use IWBs appropriately. When checked with ANOVA tests, the results showed that for this specific question there is a weak significant relation between liking to use IWBs and age except the group of the oldest students (25+). Younger learners, who were between 6 and 14 years old, strongly agreed that they like using IWBs, whereas adult learners disagreed with this idea.

EFL Teachers' Actual Use of IWB Technology

Three hours of observation in different institutions revealed that the teachers and the students are easily able to use the basic functions of IWBs, such as highlighting, writing with the special pen, saving the generated materials, searching on the Internet, and playing audio and visual files. IWBs' benefit of reducing time spent in teacher's writing in the classroom (Levy, 2002) was observed in one class, where the teacher was presenting ready-made sample paragraphs and letting the students work on them. If she had been using a traditional whiteboard, the teacher would have had to take the time to write a paragraph on the board, or else distribute a worksheet, which would not have provided an opportunity to look at and highlight the text for everyone to see. Another important benefit of IWBs observed was changing the pages (screens) without erasing the previously written materials. When a page was full of examples and answers, the teacher was able to simply open new pages. This feature, also unique to IWBs, saves time and allows teachers to turn back to previous examples as well since all the pages are saved. Although some of these functions can be seen with OHPs, it takes more time to back and forth between different kinds of resources and highligting function is very easy and flexible with IWB technology. It was also observed in at least one instance how students can search using the IWB for unknown words and present not only Turkish and English meanings of the word, but also allow the whole class to listen to the pronunciation of the word. Although there are other features such as using flipcharts, overwriting or editing a student's written work on the IWB screen, some of which can be experienced with the help of subject specific software programs designed for course books, the researcher did not witness use of these in the observed lessons. These software programs, for example, allow the students to see all the pages of the book on the IWB screen so that they can follow the lesson from the IWB screen and the teacher can involve all the students at the same time easily. These programs also provide a variety of exercises and activities that can be exploited by the teachers. The literature on IWBs in the area of language instruction does not provide empirical information about specially designed software programs since they are fairly new and only two publishers prepare these kinds of software programs. However, in Moss et al.(2007), it was found that many English teachers have difficulty in finding resources, whereas math and science teachers can easily access resources since they are using subject specific software.

Pedagogical Implications of the Study

The results of this study suggest that simply providing IWBs in some or all classrooms does not guarantee their use in language instruction as it was found out during the research. The students in the institutions where there is only one IWB-equipped classroom complain that they have experienced this technology only once or twice a semester. This lack of exposure may come from concrete problems such as lack of time or inability to schedule access to the IWB classroom, or it may come from the teachers' unwillingness to try this new technology and therefore reluctance to bring his/her students to the IWB classroom. In especially crowded schools with one IWB classroom, it will be very difficult to schedule who will use it when. The solution to this problem can be installing IWBs into more classrooms or administrators' planning equal schedules to make it possible for every class to benefit from this technology. In addition, teachers may not only face some first-order barriers such as lack of equipment and time, but also second-order barriers such as lack of confidence (Ertmer, Addison, Lane, Ross and Woods, 1999). Through professional guidance and assistance, these second-order barriers can be overcome and teachers may feel more confident and eager to benefit from this technology. Thus, administrators should arrange focus meetings with experienced teachers in using IWBs, establish a kind of sharing network among teachers in terms of materials, resources, and advice on IWB use, and encourage teachers to exploit this technology on their own with the help of experienced colleagues.

Another important and related issue is the need for training. As Hall and Higgins (2005) stated in their study, training sessions should be regular and should be viewed as a continuous process so that teachers can improve their ICT skills in order to use IWBs efficiently. This issue is also mentioned in Smith et al. (2005), where they note that in order to use IWBs to their full potential, there is a need for adequate training because inexperienced manipulations of IWB features decrease the value of this technology. Additional coaching personnel and time could be beneficial on a one to one basis and administrators can arrange training sessions that could be helpful for teachers to overcome their barriers and be more confident in using IWB technology. However, my research findings indicate that more than one third of the teachers responded that they can teach with IWBs without special training. This may show that the teachers who are interested and good at ICT skills can easily adapt themselves to IWB technology. Therefore, training could be provided by administrators according to the individuals' technological knowledge, experience, and their individual needs to exploit this technology in education.

Since most of the teachers in this study agreed that IWB technology is a good supplement for teaching, and both students and teachers have positive attitudes towards this technology, it can be argued that IWBs should be involved in the teaching process as much as possible. Although it depends on the institutions' budgets, once the decision is made to use IWBs, ideally it is advisable to install them in every classroom so that students do not have to change classrooms for IWB-based lessons. If this is not financially possible, there can be at least two or three classrooms that are equipped with IWBs. In this case, it should be ensured that students be able to find the opportunity to go to those classrooms as much as possible. Students in this study complained that they can only rarely go to the "smart class", which prevents them from experiencing and benefiting from this technology.

It should also be reminded that some publishers prepare IWB-based materials and there are a wide variety of free resources on the Internet suitable for IWB use. Teachers and administrators may wish to contact the publishers for IWB-based materials, on the condition that they choose certain course books whose materials are ready for IWB use, or search the Internet to find extra materials. On a cautionary note, since in most cases a committee, not individual teachers, decides on the books to be used in an institution, a teacher who wants to use this technology with ready-made materials may not find this opportunity. Another potential problem with using ready-made materials is that not many books are prepared with software programs, which would limit the teachers' choice if they want to benefit from these software programs. If they find the opportunity to choose course books provided with IWB software programs, teachers may get help in the exhausting process of preparing extra materials for the class and save time by using these materials.

As a last point, educators and administrators should not simply rush to buy IWBs before purchasing one. They should search for and be informed about the different features of each IWB. Although most IWBs share similar features, some of them have distinctive functions and allow more interactive opportunities during the lessons, a particularly important aspect for language teaching. After the comparison of different trademarks, the cost of this technology should also be considered. If more classrooms are intended to be equipped with IWBs, low cost IWBs could be appropriate, whereas if this technology is going to be installed in just a few classrooms, more functionally active IWBs can be chosen. It should also be noted that the size of the IWBs is also important, for instance, in large classrooms, bigger sizes would be more appropriate.

Limitations of the Study

In this study, thirteen educational institutions were surveyed, ranging from primary schools to universities. Although there are several more institutions currently using IWB technology in Turkey, time, travel constraints, and willingness to take part in this study reduced the number of institutions involved. In addition, in some institutions, there were IWBs, but they had not been installed yet, so those institutions were not included in this study. In one of the institutions surveyed, IWBs have been used for more than four years, but the rest of the institutions have been using this technology for only one year on average. This meant that in some cases students and teachers were basing their opinions on only limited exposure – a fact which no doubt led to the high "no idea" response rate for some questions. It should also be taken into consideration that in many institutions in Turkey, IWBs are used more in subject classes such as math, science, and geography. Restricting the study to institutions in which IWBs are used in language classrooms also meant that the number of institutions included in this study is far fewer than the total number of institutions currently using IWBs.

Apart from one private primary school and one high school surveyed, all the institutions in this study have this technology installed in just one or two classrooms. This limited accessibility again may have negatively influenced the extent to which IWBs are used since teachers find it difficult to share the same classroom among them. As noted above, this also meant that students and teachers in many cases did not have a great deal of exposure to lessons with IWBs, and at times could not comment on this technology appropriately. If all the participants in this study had had more experience with IWBs, they might have agreed or disagreed with the statements more easily.

The number of lessons observed in different institutions to see the actual use of IWBs in English classes was also limited. Again, time and travel constraints did not make it possible to include more observations in this study. In addition, some institutions did not consent to having

73

their teachers observed during the lessons and did not allow videorecording. Similarly, the study is limited by the few interviews with administrators, but time constraints did not allow for more.

Suggestions for Further Research

This study investigated the attitudes of students, administrators, and teachers towards the use of IWBs, factors affecting their attitudes, and the ways that EFL teachers use IWBs. Although this study includes some qualitative data, more classroom observations can be carried out to investigate to what extent teachers benefit from the potential of this technology as claimed in the literature. Such a study, if conducted in a longitudinal manner, could attempt to confirm the finding in this study that greater use correlates to more positive attitudes. As one administrator in this study pointed out, IWBs may help improve classroom interaction because the teachers do not need to turn their backs on the class. Given the importance of interaction in language learning settings, it could be the particular focus of a classroom-based research study to look at whether or how IWB use contributes to classroom interaction specifically.

The effectiveness of this technology in language instruction settings should also be examined. Although IWBs are claimed to have an impact on learning in the short term, this has not yet been confirmed. It should be checked and seen what are exactly the real contributions of this technology through experimental studies in language learning settings. If not much contribution to learning is found, investment in this technology could be questioned and investors might rethink before purchasing this expensive technology.

Conclusion

The findings of this study revealed that both students and teachers have positive attitudes towards IWB use in English language classes. IWB-based lessons are perceived as more interesting and enjoyable by both the students and teachers. In IWB-based lessons, students are more motivated and participate in the activities more. These reported contributions of IWBs may be significant for the increase of the quality of education. Although there can occur technical problems and IWBs have some drawbacks, this technology seems to be welcomed and appreciated by both students and teachers. What must be done for the effective use of this technology is that the teachers should have access to adequate training and should be provided with technical and material-based support. Since the students are already eager to use and benefit from this technology, Turkish educational institutions should be encouraged to try and provide at least a few classrooms installed with this technology if we do not want to fall behind technologically developed countries, where education goes hand in hand with technology. It should also be noted that once the teachers and students have felt the difference and benefits of this technology, they are likely to become more enthusiastic about using it. Since technology eases our lives in many areas, education may also benefit from its potential, and in this way, teaching and learning environments can be enhanced.

REFERENCES

Ahmad, K., Corbett, G., Rogers, M., & Sussex, R. (1985). *Computers, language learning and language teaching.* Cambridge: Cambridge University Press.

Alessi, S. M., & Trollip, S. R. (1991). *Computer-based instruction: Methods and development.* New Jersey: Prentice Hall.

Arkın, E. İ. (2003). *Teachers' attitudes towards computer technology use in vocabulary instruction.* Unpublished Master's thesis, Bilkent University, Ankara.

Beatty, K. (2003). *Teaching and researching computer-assisted language learning.* London: Pearson Education.

Bebell, D., O'Conner, K., O'Dwyer, L., & Russell, M. (2003). Examining teacher technology use implications for pre-service and in-service teacher preparation. *Journal of Teacher Education, 54.*

Beckman, L. O. (1999). Classroom practice: Authentic audience on the Internet. In Egbert, Hanson-Smith (Ed.), *CALL Environments: Research, practice, and critical issues.* Virginia: TESOL.

BECTA (2003a). *What the research says about ICT and motivation.* Retrieved 20 January 2008 from www.becta.org.uk.

BECTA (2003b). *What the research says about interactive whiteboards.* Retrieved 17 January 2008 from www.becta.org.uk.

BECTA (2004). *What the research says about using ICT in modern foreign languages.* Retrieved 29 June 2008 from http://partners.becta.org.uk/upload-dir/downloads/page_documents/research/wtrs_mfl.pdf.

BECTA (2005). *Evaluation of curriculum online: Emerging findings from the third survey of schools.* Retrieved 5 February 2008 from www.becta.org.uk.

Beeland, W. D. (2002). Student engagement, visual learning and technology: Can interactive whiteboards help? Retrieved 30 July 2008 from http://chiron.valdosta.edu/are/Artmanscrpt/vol1no1/beeland_am.pdf

Bell, M. A. (2002). Why use an interactive whiteboard? A baker's dozen reasons! *Teachers.Net Gazette.* Retrieved 25 March 2008 from http://teachers.net/gazette/JAN02/mabell.html

Berge, Z., & Collins, M. (1995). Computer-mediated communication and the online classroom in distance learning. *Computer-Mediated Communication Magazine, 2,* 6-12.

Birmingham, P., Davies, C., Greiffenhagen, C. (2002). Turn to face the bard: Making sense of three-way interactions between teacher, pupils and technology in the classroom. *Education, Communication & Information, 2.* Retrieved 25 July 2008 from *http://search.ebscohost.com/login.aspx?direct=true&db=a9h&AN=9162641&site=ehost-live*

Boswood, T. (1997). *New ways of using computers in language teaching*. Alexandria, Va.: Teachers of English to Speakers of Other Languages.

Boulos, M. N. K., Maramba, I., & Wheeler, S. (2006). Wikis, blogs and podcasts: A new generation of Web-based tools for virtual collaborative clinical practice and education. *BMC Medical Education, 6*, 41-41.

Celce-Murcia, M. (2001). *Teaching English as a second or foreign language*. Boston: Heinle & Heinle.

Chapelle, C. (2001). *Computer applications in second language acquisition : Foundations for teaching, testing and research*. Cambridge: Cambridge University Press.

Copley, J. (2007). Audio and video podcasts of lectures for campus-based students: Production and evaluation of student use. *Innovations in Education and Teaching International, 44*(4), 387–399.

Costanzo, W. V. (1989). *The electronic text: Learning to write, read and reason with computers*. New York: Educational Technology Publications.

Criss, K. (2006). Disadvantages of computers in the classroom. Retrieved from http://ezinearticles.com/?Disadvantages-of-Computers-in-the-Classroom&id=175360

Cuthell, J. P. (2005). *The impact of interactive whiteboards on teaching, learning and attainment*. Paper presented at the Proceedings of Society for Information Technology and Teacher Education International Conference 2005.

Dexter, S. L., Anderson, R. E., & Becker, H. J. (1999). Teachers' views of computers as catalysts for changes in their teaching practice. *Journal of Research on Computing in Education, 31*(3).

DfES (2004b). *Interactive whiteboards*. Retrieved 27 December 2007 from www.teachernet.gov.uk/educationoverview/briefing/currentstrategy/interactivewhiteboards/.

Dudeney, G., & Hockly, N. (2007). *How to teach English with technology*. Essex: Pearson Longman.

Ertmer, P. A., Addison, P., Lane, M., Ross, E., & Woods, D. (1999). Examining teachers' beliefs about the role of technology in the elementary classroom. *Journal of Research on Computing in Education, 32*(1), 54-72.

Gerard, F. (1999). *Using SMART Board in foreign language classrooms*. Paper presented at the Society for Information Technology and Teacher Education International Conference.

Glover, D., & Miller, D. (2001). Running with technology: The pedagogic impact of the large scale introduction of interactive whiteboards in one secondary school. *Journal of Information Technology for Teacher Education, 10*(3), 257-276.

Glover, D., Miller, D., Averis, D., Door, V. (2007). The evolution of an effective pedagogy for teachers using the interactive whiteboard in mathematics and modern languages: An empirical analysis from the secondary sector. *Learning, Media and Technology, 32(1)*, 5-20.

Goodison, T. (2003). Integrating ICT in the classroom: A case study of two contrasting lessons. *British Journal of Educational Technology, 34*(5), 549 – 566.

Gray, C., Hagger-Vaughan, L., Pilkington, R., & Tomkins, S.-A. (2005). The pros and cons of interactive whiteboards in relation to the key stage 3 strategy and framework. *Language Learning Journal, 32*(1), 38-44.

Hall, I., & Higgins, S. (2005). Primary school students' perceptions of interactive whiteboards. *Journal of Computer Assisted Learning, 21*(2), 102-117.

Hammersley, B. (2004). Audible revolution. *The Guardian*. Retrieved 25 July 2008 from http://technology.guardian.co.uk/online/story/0,3605,1145689,00.html

Harris, N. (2005). Interactive whiteboards: ELT's next big thing? *Modern English Teacher, 14*(2), 61-68.

Higgins, S., Beauchamp, G., Miller, D. (2007). Reviewing the literature on interactive whiteboards. *Learning, Media, & Technology, 32*, 213-225.

Hodge, S., & Anderson, B. (2007). Teaching and learning with an interactive whiteboard: A teacher's journey. *Learning, Media and Technology, 32*(3), 271-282.

Howie, S. H. (1989). *Reading, writing, and computers : Planning for integration*. London: Allyn and Bacon.

Jung, H.-J., & Kim, S. H. (2004). Opportunities in technology-enhanced language learning (TELL) classroom environments. *Teaching English With Technology, 4*(4).

Kennewell, S., & Beauchamp, G. (2007). The features of interactive whiteboards and their influence on learning. *Learning, Media and Technology, 32*(3), 227-241.

Kennewell, S., & Morgan, A. (2003). *Student teachers' experiences and attitudes towards using interactive whiteboards in the teaching and learning of young children*. Paper presented at the Proceedings of the International Federation for Information Processing Working Group 3.5 Open Conference on Young Children and Learning Technologies. Retrieved 18 May 2008 from http://portal.acm.org/citation.cfm?id=1082070#

Kennewell, S. (2001). Interactive whiteboards – yet another solution looking for a problem to solve. *Information Technology in Teacher Education, 39*, 3-6.

Kenning, M. J., & Kenning, M. M. (1983). *An introduction to computer-assisted language learning*. Oxford: Oxford University Press.

Kent, P. (2004). E-teaching with interactive whiteboards. *Administrator 26 (1)*. Retrieved 13 January 2008 from http://www.iwb.net.au/public/content/ViewCategory.aspx?id=34

Lai, C.-C., & Kritsonis, W. A. (2006). The Advantages and Disadvantages of Computer

Technology in Second Language Acquisition. *National Journal for Publishing and Mentoring Doctoral Student Research, 3 (1).*

Lee, B., & Boyle, M. (2004). Teachers tell their story: Interactive whiteboards at Richardson Primary School.

Lee, K. (2000). English teachers' barriers to the use of computer-assisted language learning. *The Internet TESL Journal, 6*(12).

Levy, M. (1997). *Computer-assisted language learning: Context and conceptualization.* Oxford: Clarendon Press.

Levy, P. (2002). *Interactive whiteboards in learning and teaching in two Sheffield schools: A developmental study.* Retrieved 12 March 2008 from http://dis.shef.ac.uk/eirg/projects/wboards.htm.

Lin, A. (2003). An initial study on EFL learners' attitude towards multimedia application in language learning. *Teaching English with Technology (IATEFL Poland), 3*(2).

Martin, S. (2007). Interactive whiteboards and talking books: A new approach to teaching children to write? *Literacy (formerly called Reading), 41*(1), 26-34.

May, T. (2005). Brief thoughts about IT in language education. *Teaching English with Technology (IATEFL Poland) , 5*(2). Retrieved 20 June 2008 from http://www.iatefl.org.pl/call/j_article21.htm.

Moss, G., Jewitt, C., Levaäiç, R., Armstrong, V., Cardini, A., & Castle, F. (2007). *The interactive whiteboards, pedagogy and pupil performance evaluation.* Retrieved 12 January 2008 from www.dfes.gov.uk/research/data/uploadfiles/RR816.pdf.

Passey, D., & Rogers, C. (2004). *The motivational effect of ICT on pupils.* Retrieved 19 April 2008 from http://www.dfes.gov.uk/research/data/uploadfiles/RR523new.pdf.

Pekel, N. (1997). *Students' attitudes towards web-based independent learning at Bilkent University School of English Language.* Unpublished master's thesis, Bilkent University, Ankara.

Pennington, M. C. (1996). The power of the computer in language education. In M. C. Pennington (Ed.), *The power of CALL, pp 1-14.* Houston: Athelstan.

Robinson, G. L. (1991). Effective feedback strategies in CALL: Learning theory and empirical research. *Computer-assisted Language Learning And Testing*, 189-203.

Schmid, E. C. (2006). Investigating the use of interactive whiteboard technology in the English language classroom through the lens of a critical theory of technology. *Computer Assisted Language Learning: An International Journal, 19*(1), 47-62.

Schmid, E. C. (2007). Enhancing performance knowledge and self-esteem in classroom language learning: The potential of the ACTIVote component of interactive whiteboard technology.

System: An International Journal of Educational Technology and Applied Linguistics, 35(2), 119-133.

Schoepp, K., & Eroğul, M. (2001). Turkish EFL students' utilization of information technology outside of the classroom. *TEFL Web Journal, -.*

Schofield, J. W. (1995). *Computers and classroom culture*. Cambridge: Cambridge University Press.

SDS, (2008). Interactive whiteboards. Coventry. Retrieved 20 June 2008 from http://www.sdsonline.qld.gov.au/documents/IWB%20Information%20Booklet%20-%20Education.pdf

Shin, H.-J., & Son, J.-B. (2007). EFL teachers' perceptions and perspectives on internet-assisted language teaching. *CALL-EJ Online, 8*(2).

Smith, A. (1999). Interactive whiteboard evaluation. Retrieved 27 May 2008 from http://www.mirandanet.ac.uk/pubs/smartboards.htm

Smith, B. (1997). Virtual Realia. *The Internet TESL journal, 3*(7). Retrieved 18 July 2008 from http://iteslj.org/Articles/Smith-Realia.html

Smith, H. (2001). *Smartboard evaluation: Final report*. Retrieved from http://www.kented.org.uk/ngfl/ict/IWB/whiteboards/report.html

Smith, H. J., Higgins, S., Wall, K., & Miller, J. (2005). Interactive whiteboards: Boon or bandwagon? A critical review of the literature. *Journal of Computer Assisted Learning, 21*(2), 91-101.

Summet, J., Abowd, G. D., Corso, G. M., & Rehg, J. M. (2005). *Virtual rear projection: Do shadows matter?* Paper presented at the Conference on Human Factors in Computing Systems. Retrieved 7 June 2008, from http://delivery.acm.org/10.1145/1060000/1057076/p1997-summet.pdf?key1=1057076&key2=1166745121&coll=GUIDE&dl=GUIDE&CFID=77165468&CFTOKEN=58053916

Tameside MBC. (2003). *Interim report on practice using interactive whiteboards in Tameside primary schools*. Retrieved from http://www.tameside.gov.uk/schools_grid/ict/whiteboards.pdf.

Tuzcuoğlu, U. (2000). *Teachers' attitudes towards using computer assisted language learning (CALL) in the foreign languages department at Osmangazi University*. Unpublished Master's Thesis, Bilkent University, Ankara.

Vilmi, R. (1999). CALL issues: Language learning over distance. In Egbert, Hanson-Smith (Ed.), *CALL Environments: Research, practice, and critical issues*. Virginia: TESOL.

Walker, D. (2002). White enlightening. *Times Educational Supplement*, p.19.

Wall, K., Higgins, S., Smith, H., (2005). The visual helps me understand the complicated things: Pupil views of teaching and learning with interactive whiteboards. *British Journal of Educational Technology, 36*(5), 851-867.

Warschauer, M. (2000). On-line learning in second language classrooms. In M. Warschauer & R. Kern (Eds.), Network-based language teaching: Concepts and practice (pp. 41-58). New York: Cambridge University Press.

Warschauer, M., & Healey, D. (1998). Computers and language learning: An overview. *Language Teaching, 31,* 57-71.

Weimer, M. J. (2001). *The influence of technology such as a SMART board interactive whiteboard on student motivation in the classroom.* Smarter Kid Foundation, retrieved 24 May 2008 from http://smarterkids.org/research/paper7.asp

Wood, R. (1999). Thinking about the Internet pedagogically. *Rutgers, The State University of New Jersey Campus at Camden.* Retrieved 11 April 2008 from http://www.camden.rutgers.edu/%7Ewood/pedagogy.html

APPENDIX A

Consent Form

Dear colleagues and students,

I am currently enrolled in the MA TEFL Program at Bilkent University. The aim of my research study is to investigate the attitudes of students and teachers towards the use of interactive whiteboards (IWBs) in English classes. I am also examining the similarities and differences between the perceptions of students and teachers towards the use of IWB technology and factors affecting students' and teachers' attitudes towards this technology in language instruction.

Questionnaires for students and teachers are the first phase of my study. Interviews with administrators will be the second phase of my study. Moreover, class observations will be carried out to see the actual use of IWBs in English lessons. Be sure that all the personal data provided from questionnaires, interviews, and observations will be kept strictly confidential in my reports.

If you have any questions, please do not hesitate to contact me or my thesis advisor, Dr. Julie Mathews Aydınlı.

Thank you in advance for your help and cooperation.

M. Fatih Elaziz	Dr. Julie Mathews Aydınlı
MA TEFL	MA TEFL
Bilkent University, Ankara	Bilkent University, Ankara
Tel: (090) 312 266 4066	Tel: (090) 312 290 2746
felaziz@gmail.com	julie@bilkent.edu.tr

Consent Form

I have read the above information. I hereby give my consent for the data acquired to be used by M. Fatih Elaziz in this survey.

Name:

Date:

Signature:

STUDENT QUESTIONNAIRE

Akıllı Tahta Kullanımına Yönelik Öğrenci Tutum ve Düşünce Anketi

---

Sayın katılımcı,

bu çalışma Bilkent Üniversitesinde bir yabancı dil olarak İngilizce öğretimi (MA TEFL) yüksek lisans programı bünyesinde öğrencilerin ve öğretmenlerin İngilizce derslerinde akıllı tahta kullanımına yönelik tutum ve düşüncelerini ölçmeyi amaçlamaktadır. Vereceğiniz bilgiler kesinlikle gizli tutulacak ve kendi çalışmamla sınırlı kalacaktır.

Şimdiden katkılarınızdan ve işbirliğinizden dolayı teşekkür ederim.

Bölüm I: Genel Bilgiler (Background Knowledge about the Students)

1. Yaşınız: 6-14 ☐   15-19 ☐   20-25 ☐   26 ve yukarısı ☐
2. Cinsiyetiniz: Erkek ☐   Kız ☐
3. Okul/Kurum türü:

    İlköğretim ☐   Lise ☐   Üniversite ☐   Dil Kursu ☐
4. İngilizce seviyeniz: Elementary ☐   Pre-Intermediate ☐   Intermediate ☐

    Upper-Intermediate ☐   Advanced ☐
5. Bir hafta içinde kaç saat akıllı tahta ile İngilizce dersi yapıyorsunuz?

    1-2 saat ☐   3-5 saat ☐   6-10 saat ☐   11 saat ve yukarısı ☐
6. İngilizce derslerinde en çok hangi beceriler için akıllı tahta kullanılıyor?

    Writing ☐   Speaking ☐   Reading ☐   Grammar ☐   Integrated Skills ☐

Bölüm II: Genel Tutumlar (General Attitudes)

Aşağıdaki ifadelere ne kadar katılıyorsunuz? Size en uygun olan kutuyu işaretleyiniz. (O)

Aşağıdaki tabloda sayıların anlamı şu şekildedir:

1) Kesinlikle katılmıyorum   2) Katılmıyorum   3) Fikrim yok

4) Katılıyorum   5) Kesinlikle katılıyorum

1. Öğretmenim İngilizce derslerinde akıllı tahta kullandığında daha fazla öğreniyorum. *(I learn more when my teacher uses the whiteboard in*	1	2	3	4	5

English classes.)	
2. Öğretmenimiz akıllı tahta kullandığında konuyu anlamak daha çok kolaylaşıyor. *(It is easier to understand the lesson when my teacher uses an IWB.)*	1 2 3 4 5
3. Akıllı tahta sayesinde öğretmenin yazım ve çizimleri daha anlaşılır hale geliyor. *(IWBs make the teachers' drawings and diagrams easier to see.)*	1 2 3 . 4 5
4. Akıllı tahta kullanımı ile görsel ve işitsel materyaller yabancı dil derslerini daha kolay anlamamı sağlıyor. *(Using audio and visual materials with IWBs helps me understand the language classes better.)*	1 2 3 4 5
5. Akıllı tahta sayesinde bir konuyu daha fazla ve değişik kaynaktan öğrenme imkanı buluyorum. *(I find the opportunity to learn from different sources with the use of IWBs.)*	1 2 3 4 5
6. Zaman zaman görüntü bozuklukları veya güneş ışığının yeterince engellenmemesi tahtadakileri görmemi olumsuz etkiliyor. *(Sometimes deficiencies of the IWB screen and sunlight in the classroom make it difficult to see the things on the IWB.)*	1 2 3 4 5
7. Akıllı tahtalar sıklıkla bozuluyor ve tekrar ayarlanması zaman kaybına sebep oluyor. *(IWBs often break down and recalibration causes a waste of time.)*	1 2 3 4 5
8. Sınıfın önüne çıkıp akıllı tahtayı kullanmayı seviyorum. *(I like going to the front of the class to use the IWB.)*	1 2 3 4 5
9. Akıllı tahtayı kullanmak bana zor geliyor. *(It seems difficult for me to use IWBs.)*	1 2 3 4 5
10. Akıllı tahtanın kullanıldığı dersleri tercih ederim. *(I prefer lessons that are taught with an IWB.)*	1 2 3 4 5
11. Benim çalışmamın ya da ödevimin tüm sınıfa akıllı tahta ile gösterilmesi beni rahatsız ediyor. *(It makes me uncomfortable when my work is shown to the whole class on the IWB.)*	1 2 3 4 5
12. Akıllı tahta ile ders anlatıldığında İngilizce derslerine daha fazla konsantre oluyorum. *(I concentrate better when my teacher uses an IWB in English classes.)*	1 2 3 4 5
13. Öğretmenimiz yabancı dil derslerinde akıllı tahta kullandığında derse daha fazla katılıyorum. *(I participate in language classes more when my*	1 2 3 4 5

teacher uses an IWB.)					
14. Akıllı tahtalar yabancı dil öğrenmeyi daha zevkli ve ilginç hale getiriyor. *(IWBs make language learning more interesting and exciting.)*	1	2	3	4	5
15. Akıllı tahta kullanılırken dikkatimi daha kolayca toplayabiliyor ve daha uzun süre koruyabiliyorum. *(It is easier to keep my attention when an IWB is used during the English classes.)*	1	2	3	4	5
16. Akıllı tahta kullanımı yabancı dil derslerine karşı motive olmamı kolaylaştırıyor. *(Use of an IWB makes it easier for me to be motivated during the language classes.)*	1	2	3	4	5
17. Öğretmenim akıllı tahta ile ders anlatırken çok hızlı ilerlediği için takip edemiyorum. *(When my teacher uses an IWB, I cannot keep up with the lesson because the pace of the lesson is much faster.)*	1	2	3	4	5
18. Akıllı tahta kullanımı ile dersler daha planlı ve organize hale geliyor. *(The lessons become more organized when an IWB is used.)*	1	2	3	4	5
19. Akıllı tahta zaman kazandırıyor ve dersin daha hızlı ilerlemesini sağlıyor. *(Using an IWB saves time.)*	1	2	3	4	5
20. Öğretmenlerimizin akıllı tahta kullanırkenki ders anlatımı ile normal tahtayla ders anlatırkenki öğretim tarzları ve yöntemleri aynıdır. *(There is no difference between my teacher's use of a traditional board and an IWB in terms of teaching techniques and methods.)*	1	2	3	4	5
21. Bana göre normal tahta ile akıllı tahta arasında çok büyük bir fark yok. *(I think there is not much difference between an IWB and a normal whiteboard.)*	1	2	3	4	5

Bölüm III: Ek Bilgi ve Düşünceler

1. Eklemek istediğiniz başka bir şey var mı? ....
....
....

2. Akıllı tahta kullanımı ile ilgili herhangi bir tavsiyeniz veya şikayetiniz var mı?
....
....

Teşekkürler.

TEACHER QUESTIONNAIRE

Teacher Questionnaire

Dear participant,

This study is conducted in MA TEFL Program in Bilkent University. It aims to investigate attitudes and perceptions of students and teachers towards the use of interactive whiteboards in EFL classrooms. This questionnaire for teachers is the first phase of my study. You can be sure that all the personal data provided from questionnaires will be kept strictly confidential in my reports. Thank you in advance for your help and contribution.

Section I: General Information

1. Your age: 20-25 ☐   26-30 ☐   31-35 ☐   36-40 ☐   41-45 ☐   46-Above ☐

2. Gender: Male ☐   Female ☐

3. Type of your institution/school you teach at:

   Primary ☐   High School ☐   University ☐   Language School ☐

4. Years of teaching experience:

   1-5 years ☐   6-10 years ☐   11-15 years ☐   16-20 years ☐   21- above ☐

5. How many hours do you teach with an interactive whiteboard in English classes in a week?

   1-2 hours a week ☐   3-5 hours a week ☐   6-10 hours a week ☐

   11 or more hours ☐

6. For which language skills do you use IWB technology most?

   Writing ☐   Speaking ☐   Reading ☐   Grammar ☐   Integrated Skills ☐

Section II: General Attitudes

For the following items, please circle the answers that best show your opinion. (O)

1= Strongly disagree   2= Disagree   3= No idea   4= Agree

5= Strongly agree

1. Using IWB-based resources reduces the time I spend in writing.	1	2	3	4	5
2. When using IWBs in the classroom, I spend more time for the preparation of the lesson.	1	2	3	4	5
3. I think using IWBs makes it easier to reach different sources and display them to the whole class immediately.	1	2	3	4	5

4. IWBs are beneficial to be able to save and print the materials generated during English classes.	1	2	3	4	5
5. I can give more effective explanations with the use of IWBs.	1	2	3	4	5
6. With the help of using an IWB I can easily control the whole class.	1	2	3	4	5
7. I think IWBs can be a good supplement to support English teaching.	1	2	3	4	5
8. Using IWBs makes me a more efficient language teacher.	1	2	3	4	5
9. Using IWBs makes it easier for a teacher to review, re-explain, and summarize the subject.	1	2	3	4	5
10. I like using IWB technology in my english classes.	1	2	3	4	5
11. I feel uncomfortable in front of my students while using IWB.	1	2	3	4	5
12. I have positive attitudes towards the use of IWBs in language instruction.	1	2	3	4	5
13. I have negative attitudes towards the use of IWBs in language classes.	1	2	3	4	5
14. I do not think my students are ready for this technology.	1	2	3	4	5
15. What I do in class with traditional methods is sufficient in teaching English.	1	2	3	4	5
16. I am not the type to do well with IWB-based applications.	1	2	3	4	5
17. I think IWBs make language learning more enjoyable and more interesting.	1	2	3	4	5
18. I believe that training is required to teach with IWB technology.	1	2	3	4	5
19. If I do not get sufficient training, I do not feel comfortable with using IWBs in classrooms.	1	2	3	4	5
20. I can keep my students' attention longer with the help of IWB technology in language classes.	1	2	3	4	5
21. I think IWBs increase the interaction and participation of the students in English classes.	1	2	3	4	5
22. I think my students are more motivated when I use an IWB in my English classes.	1	2	3	4	5

Section III: Additional ideas and suggestions

1. Is there any other comment you would like to add about the use of IWBs:

....

2. Any problem or suggestion about the use of IWBs: ....

....

INTERVIEW PROTOCOL

YÖNETICI GÖRÜSME SORULARI (INTERVIEW QUESTIONS)

1) İngilizce öğretmenleri için teknoloji kullanımını gerekli görüyor musunuz? *(Do you think that the use of technology is necessary for EFL teachers?)*

2) Sizce İngilizce öğretmenleri yeterince teknoloji olanaklarından faydalanıyorlar mı? *(Do you think that EFL teachers benefit from technology sufficiently?)*

3) İngilizce öğretiminde akıllı tahta kullanımına ne şekilde destek veriyorsunuz? *(In what ways do you support the use of IWBs in language instruction?)*

4) Hangi faktörler akıllı tahta teknolojisini satın almanıza sebep oldu? *(What factors influenced you to purchase IWB technology?)*

5) Akıllı tahta kullanımı ile ilgili olarak öğretmenlerin karşılaştığı en yaygın problemler nelerdir? *(What are the most common problems EFL teachers face when using IWBs?)*

6) Sizce akıllı tahta teknolojisi İngilizce öğretiminde ne gibi faydalar sağlayabilir? *(In your opinion, what could be the benefits of IWBs in English teaching settings?)*

SAMPLE TRANSCRIPT OF INTERVIEW

Interviewer: This is an interview about the use of interactive whiteboards in language instruction. I want to ask some questions. First of all, do you think that the use of technology is necessary for EFL teachers?

Interviewee: Of course, it is necessary, but it should serve a purpose. For example, technology should not used for only entertainment and it should be used with an intention related to teaching.

Interviewer: Do you think that EFL teachers benefit from technology sufficiently?

Interviewee: Yes, our staff benefit from technology sufficiently according to their needs. They also support each other using technological devices and materials.

Interviewer: Do they have intrinsic motivation or feel that technology use is an obligation?

Interviewee: At first, it was not easy to be accustomed to technology use, but once the teachers have been accustomed to the use of technology and have received positive feedback from their students, they liked technology use in the lessons. Thus, it was a mutual process between the students and the teachers. Even though the teachers were hesitant at first, the role of decreasing the teachers' burden helped them like the technology, so they love using technology now.

Interviewer: As an administrator, in what ways do you support the use of IWBs? Your staff have started to use this technology, but do you think that they need more support?

Interviewee: When our staff encounter technical problems, we support technical assistance. The school administration provides a great deal of help regarding installation of the IWB system and technical problems. Moreover, publishers have also helped us. I do not think we have faced many problems so far. When the batteries of pens are run out of energy, we supply new ones. If there is a problem with sound system, we get technical assistance from the technicians. I must also note that if schools do not have proper technological infrastructure, they may have problems about technology use.

...

Interviewer: Have your staff had special training before using this technology?

Interviewee: One of our teachers, as far as I know, has taken a special training. And she planned a training program for her colleagues. Each of our teachers, either one by one or in groups of two, got training from her. She also helped the teachers when they had problems with the system and the IWBs. For instance, some teachers had problems with the pen, so that teacher showed them how to use it. I can say that we have overcome all problems so far and the system is working well now.

...

Interviewer: What factors influenced you to purchase IWB technology? Of course, you did not purchase IWBs personally, but what factors were influential on the manager of this institution? Interviewee: When I started to work here, it had already been decided. I taught English using this book (Face2Face) without benefitting from IWB technology last year. In order to see the difference between traditional teaching and IWB-based teaching, I need to teach English with an IWB using this book ths year. According to the feedback received from my staff, IWB-based lessons are nicer, and more interesting then traditional English classes. If I had had a chance to teach with an IWB last year, I would express my thoughts more clearly now. Before the decision process about IWB installation, our administration asked our staff's opinions about this technology. After the program coordinators have examined this technology, they also informed the administration about the benefits of IWBs. After a formal meeting in which all the stakeholders expressed their thoughts, the administration was persuaded to purchase IWB technology.

APPENDIX F

CHECKLIST FOR IWB USE IN CLASS

1. Teachers or student (T/S) highlights a text or parts of a text with different colors. ☐

2. T/S can use his/her finger to draw or highlight something on the IWB screen. ☐

3. T/S searches for something on the Internet. ... ☐

4. T uses a subject specific software program during the lesson. ☐

5. T/S hides and reveals a text or a part of a text or image. ☐

6. T/S uses drag and drop function of the IWB. ☐

7. T/S plays audio and video files. ☐

8. T/S writes on the board using a stylus pen. ☐

9. T/S saves written pages by clicking on the next icon. ☐

10. T/S prints out the students' work and distribute them to the whole class. ☐

11. T/S uses scanner to display the students' written product on the IWB. ☐

12. T/S uses a wireless keyboard for writing on the board. ☐

13. Ss have special hand-held tools for voting right or wrong answers in a test or exercise. ☐

14. T navigates the texts and images from the board screen, not from the desktop or laptop computer. ☐

15. T/S edits a student's written work on the board underlying, highlighting, or erasing. ☐

16. Other uses. ☐

17. Problems

   a) board is difficult to see due to sun light ☐

   b) computer breaks down or jams ☐

   c) teacher is not confident in using the IWB ☐

Printed in Great Britain
by Amazon